PROJECT: NECKLACES

KALMBACH BOOKS

Kalmbach Books
21027 Crossroads Circle
Waukesha, Wisconsin 53186
www.Kalmbach.com/Books

Published in 2013
17 16 15 14 13   1 2 3 4 5

Manufactured in the United States of America

ISBN: 978-087116-751-4
EISBN: 978-1-62700-061-1

The material in this book has appeared previously in *Bead&Button* magazine. Bead&Button is registered as a trademark.

Editor: Erica Swanson
Art Director: Carole Ross
Illustrator: Kellie Jaeger
Photographers: James Forbes and William Zuback

Publisher's Cataloging-in-Publication Data
Project. Necklaces / [compiled by Kalmbach Books ; editor: Erica Swanson].

   p. : col. ill. ; cm. — (Project (Kalmbach Books))

"30 designs using beads, wire, chain, and more"—Cover.

"The material in this book has appeared previously in Bead&Button magazine."—T.p. verso.

Issued also as an ebook.
ISBN: 978-0-87116-751-4

1. Necklaces—Handbooks, manuals, etc. 2. Beadwork—Handbooks, manuals, etc. 3. Wire jewelry—Handbooks, manuals, etc. 4. Jewelry making—Handbooks, manuals, etc. I. Swanson, Erica. II. Kalmbach Publishing Company. III. Title: Necklaces IV. Title: Bead&Button magazine.

TT860 .P76 2013
745.594/2

Contents

Introduction

There's nothing quite like a necklace to complete an outfit. Whether you're dressing up a T-shirt and jeans or finishing off a glamorous evening look, a beautiful necklace is the perfect accompaniment for any ensemble.

That's where *Project: Necklaces* comes in. With 30 gorgeous pieces, you'll find necklaces to suit any style. This collection of projects represents the wide range of looks and skills that can be combined to create necklaces of all kinds.

The four chapters in this book are organized by technique: stringing, beadweaving with single stitches, combining techniques, and wirework. As you work, refer to the basic tools, materials, and techniques if necessary.

So, go ahead—adorn your neck with glittering crystals, gorgeous gemstones, and snappy seed beads! You'll find it all within the pages of *Project: Necklaces*.

Tools & Materials

Excellent tools and materials for making jewelry are available in bead and craft stores, through catalogs, and on the Internet. Here are the essential supplies you'll need for the projects in this book.

TOOLS

Chainnose pliers have smooth, flat inner jaws, and the tips taper to a point. Use them for gripping, bending wire, and for opening and closing loops and jump rings.

Roundnose pliers have smooth, tapered, conical jaws used to make loops. The closer to the tip you work, the smaller the loop will be.

Use the front of a **wire cutters'** blades to make a pointed cut and the back of the blades to make a flat cut. Do not use your jewelry-grade wire cutters on memory wire, which is extremely hard; use heavy-duty wire cutters, or bend the memory wire back and forth until it breaks.

Crimping pliers have two grooves in their jaws that are used to fold or roll a crimp bead into a compact shape.

Make it easier to open split rings by inserting the curved jaw of **split-ring pliers** between the wires.

Beading needles are coded by size. The higher the number, the finer the beading needle. Unlike sewing needles, the eye of a beading needle is almost as narrow as its shaft. In addition to the size of the bead, the number of times you will pass through the bead also affects the needle size that you will use. If you will pass through a bead multiple times, you need to use a thinner needle.

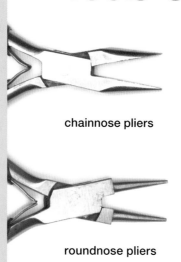

chainnose pliers

roundnose pliers

wire cutters

crimping pliers

split-ring pliers

beading needles

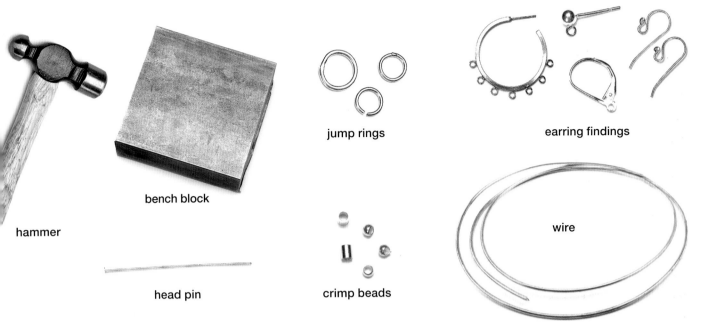

jump rings

earring findings

hammer

bench block

head pin

crimp beads

wire

A **hammer** is used to harden wire or texture metal. Any hammer with a flat head will work, as long as the head is free of nicks that could mar your metal. The light ball-peen hammer shown here is one of the most commonly used hammers for jewelry making.

A **bench block** provides a hard, smooth surface on which to hammer wire and metal pieces. An **anvil** is similarly hard but has different surfaces, such as a tapered horn, to help form wire into different shapes.

FINDINGS

A **head pin** looks like a long, blunt, thick sewing pin. It has a flat or decorative head on one end to keep beads on. Head pins come in different metals, diameters (or gauges), and lengths.

A **jump ring** is used to connect two loops. It is a small wire circle, oval, or decorative shape that is either soldered closed or comes with a split so you can twist the jump ring open and closed.

Crimp beads and tubes are large-hole, thin-walled metal beads designed to be flattened or crimped into a tight roll. Use them when stringing jewelry on flexible beading wire. **Crimp bead covers** provide a way to hide your crimps by covering them with a finding that mimics the look of a small bead.

Earring findings come in a huge variety of metals and styles, including post, French hook, hoop, and leverback. You will almost always want a loop (or loops) on earring findings so you can attach beads or beadwork.

WIRE

Wire is available in a number of materials and finishes, including brass, gold, gold-filled, gold-plated, fine silver, sterling silver, anodized niobium (chemically colored wire), and copper. Brass, copper, and craft wire are packaged in 10- to 40-yd. (9.1–37 m) spools, while gold, silver, and niobium are sold by the foot or ounce. Wire thickness is measured by gauge — the higher the gauge number, the thinner the wire. It is available in varying hardnesses (dead-soft, half-hard, and hard) and shapes (round, half-round, square, and others).

STITCHING & STRINGING MATERIALS

Thread comes in many sizes and strengths. Size (diameter or thickness) is designated by a letter or number. OO, O, and A are the thinnest threads; B, D, E, F, and FF are subsequently thicker.

Plied gel-spun polyethylene (GSP), such as Power Pro or DandyLine, is made from polyethylene fibers that have been spun into two or more threads that are braided together. It is

almost unbreakable, doesn't stretch, and resists fraying. The thickness can make it difficult to make multiple passes through a bead. It is ideal for stitching with larger beads, such as pressed glass and crystals. **Parallel filament GSP**, such as Fireline, is a single-ply thread made from spun and bonded polyethylene fibers. Because it's thin and strong, it's best for stitching with small seed beads.

Other threads are available, including **parallel filament nylon**, such as Nymo or C-Lon, and **pre-conditioned parallel filament nylon**, like K.O. or One-G (best used in beadweaving and bead embroidery); **plied nylon thread**, such as Silamide (good for twisted fringe, bead crochet, and beadwork that needs a lot of body); and **polyester thread**, such as Gutermann (best for bead crochet or bead embroidery when the thread must match the fabric).

Flexible beading wire is composed of steel wires twisted together and covered with nylon. This wire is much stronger than thread and does not stretch. The higher the number of inner strands (between three and 49), the more flexible and kink-resistant the wire. It is available in a variety of sizes and colors. Use .014 and .015 for most gemstones, crystals, and glass beads. Use thicker varieties (.018, .019, and .024) for heavy beads or nuggets. Use thinner wire (.010 and .012) for lightweight pieces and beads with very small holes, such as pearls.

Tools & Materials

BEADS

Many of the projects in this book will call for **seed beads** as the main elements of the design. The most common and highest-quality seed beads are manufactured in Japan or the Czech Republic. These seed beads are the most uniform and predictable in size, shape, and hole size. Bead sizes are written as a number with a symbol, such as 11/0 or 11º (pronounced "eleven aught"). Sizes range from 2º (6 mm) to 24º (smaller than 1 mm) — the higher the number, the smaller the bead. The most common seed bead size is 11º, but most suppliers carry sizes ranging from 6º to 15º. Seed beads smaller than 15º are difficult to work with as their holes are tiny, and thus are rarely used and very hard to find.

Japanese cylinder beads, which are sold under the brand names Delicas, Treasures, or Aikos, are very consistent in shape and size. Unlike the standard round seed bead, they're shaped like little tubes and have very large, round holes and straight sides. They create an even surface texture when stitched together in beadwork. These beads are also sold in tubes or packages by weight. In addition to round and cylinder beads, there are several other seed bead shapes: **Hex-cut beads** are similar to cylinder beads, but instead of a smooth, round exterior, they have six sides. **Triangle beads** have three sides, and **cube beads** have four. **Bugle beads** are long, thin tubes that can range in size from 2–30 mm long. You might also find tiny teardrop-shaped beads, called **drops** or **fringe drops**, and **magatamas**. Cube, drop, and bugle beads are sold by size, measured in millimeters (mm) rather than aught size.

Some projects may also use a variety of **accent beads** to embellish your pieces, including **crystals**, **gemstones**, **fire-polished beads**, and **pearls**, to name only a few types.

seed beads

cube beads

triangle beads

drop beads

twisted bugle beads

hex-cut beads

Czech seed beads

Techniques

THREAD AND KNOTS

Adding thread
To add a thread, sew into the beadwork several rows or rounds prior to the point where the last bead was added, leaving a short tail. Follow the thread path of the stitch, tying a few half-hitch knots (see "Half-hitch knot") between beads as you go, and exit where the last stitch ended. Trim the short tail.

Conditioning thread
Use beeswax or microcrystalline wax (not candle wax or paraffin) or Thread Heaven to condition nylon beading thread and Fireline. Wax smooths nylon fibers and adds tackiness that will stiffen your beadwork slightly. Thread Heaven adds a static charge that causes the thread to repel itself, so don't use it with doubled thread. Both conditioners help thread resist wear. To condition, stretch nylon thread to remove the curl (Fireline doesn't stretch). Lay the thread or Fireline on top of the conditioner, hold it in place with your thumb or finger, and pull the thread through the conditioner.

Ending thread
To end a thread, sew back through the last few rows or rounds of beadwork, following the thread path of the stitch and tying two or three half-hitch knots (see "Half-hitch knot") between beads as you go. Sew through a few beads after the last knot, and trim the thread.

Stop bead

Use a stop bead to secure beads temporarily when you begin stitching. Choose a bead that is different from the beads in your project. Pick up the stop bead, leaving the desired length tail. Sew through the stop bead again in the same direction, making sure you don't split the thread. If desired, sew through it one more time for added security.

Half-hitch knot

Pass the needle under the thread bridge between two beads, and pull gently until a loop forms. Cross back over the thread between the beads, sew through the loop, and pull gently to draw the knot into the beadwork.

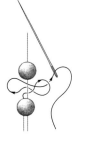

Overhand knot

Make a loop with the thread. Pull the tail through the loop, and tighten.

Square knot

[1] Cross one end of the thread over and under the other end. Pull both ends to tighten the first half of the knot.
[2] Cross the first end of the thread over and under the other end. Pull both ends to tighten the knot.

Surgeon's knot

[1] Cross one end of the thread over and under the other twice. Pull both ends to tighten the first half of the knot.
[2] Cross the first end of the thread over and under the other end. Pull both ends to tighten the knot.

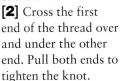

Brick stitch

[1] To work the typical method, which results in progressively decreasing rows, work the first row in ladder stitch (see "Ladder stitch") to the desired length, exiting the top of the last bead added.

[2] Pick up two beads, sew under the thread bridge between the second and third beads in the previous row, and sew back up through the second bead added. To secure this first stitch, sew down through the first bead and back up through the second bead.
[3] For the remaining stitches in the row, pick up one bead per stitch, sew under the thread bridge between the next two beads in the previous row, and sew back up through the new bead.

Increasing

To increase at the start of the row, repeat step 1 above, then repeat step 2, but sew under the thread bridge between the first and second beads in the previous row. To increase at the end of the row, work two stitches off of the thread bridge between the last two beads in the previous row.

Herringbone stitch
Flat

[1] Work the first row in ladder stitch (see "Ladder stitch") to the desired length, exiting the top of an end bead in the ladder.
[2] Pick up two beads, and sew down through the next bead in the previous row (a–b). Sew up through the following bead in the previous row, pick up two beads, and sew down through the next bead (b–c). Repeat across the first row.

[3] To turn to start the next row, sew down through the end bead in the previous row and back through the last bead of the pair just added (a–b). Pick up two beads, sew down through the next bead in the previous row, and sew up through the following bead (b–c). Continue adding pairs of beads across the row.

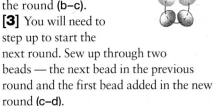

Tubular

[1] Work a row of ladder stitch (see "Ladder stitch") to the desired length using an even number of beads. Form it into a ring to create the first round (see "Ladder stitch: Forming a ring"). Your thread should exit the top of a bead.
[2] Pick up two beads, sew down through the next bead in the previous round (a–b), and sew up through the following bead. Repeat to complete the round (b–c).
[3] You will need to step up to start the next round. Sew up through two beads — the next bead in the previous round and the first bead added in the new round (c–d).
[4] Continue adding two beads per stitch. As you work, snug up the beads to form a tube, and step up at the end of each round until your rope is the desired length.

Ladder stitch
Making a ladder

[1] Pick up two beads, and sew through them both again, positioning the beads side by side so that their holes are parallel (a–b).
[2] Add subsequent beads by picking up one bead, sewing through the previous bead, then sewing through the new bead (b–c). Continue for the desired length. This technique produces

uneven tension, which you can correct by zigzagging back through the beads in the opposite direction or by choosing the "Crossweave method" or "Alternative method."

Crossweave method
[1] Thread a needle on each end of a length of thread, and center a bead.
[2] Working in crossweave technique, pick up a bead with one needle, and cross the other needle through it **(a–b and aa–bb)**. Add all subsequent beads in the same manner.

Alternative method
[1] Pick up all the beads you need to reach the length your project requires. Fold the last two beads so they are parallel, and sew through the second-to-last bead again in the same direction **(a–b)**.
[2] Fold the next loose bead so it sits parallel to the previous bead in the ladder, and sew through the loose bead in the same direction **(a–b)**. Continue sewing back through each bead until you exit the last bead of the ladder.

Forming a ring
With your thread exiting the last bead in the ladder, sew through the first bead and then through the last bead again. If using the "Crossweave method" or "Alternative method" of ladder

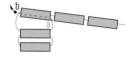

stitch, cross the threads from the last bead in the ladder through the first bead in the ladder.

Peyote stitch
Flat even-count
[1] Pick up an even number of beads, leaving the desired length tail **(a–b)**. These beads will shift to form the first two rows as the third row is added.
[2] To begin row 3, pick up a bead, skip the last bead added in the previous step, and sew back through the next bead, working toward the tail **(b–c)**.

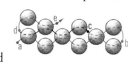

For each stitch, pick up a bead, skip a bead in the previous row, and sew through the next bead until you reach the first bead picked up in step 1 **(c–d)**. The beads added in this row are higher than the previous rows and are referred to as "up-beads."
[3] For each stitch in subsequent rows, pick up a bead, and sew through the next up-bead in the previous row **(d–e)**. To count peyote stitch rows, count the total number of beads along both straight edges.

Tubular
Tubular peyote stitch follows the same stitching pattern as flat peyote, but instead of sewing back and forth, you work in rounds.
[1] Start with an even number of beads tied into a ring (see "Square knot").
[2] Sew through the first bead in the ring. Pick up a bead, skip a bead in the ring, and sew through the next bead. Repeat to complete the round.

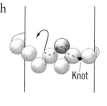

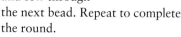

[3] To step up to start the next round, sew through the first bead added in round 3 **(a–b)**. Pick up a bead, and sew through the next bead in round 3 **(b–c)**. Repeat to complete the round.
[4] Repeat step 3 to achieve the desired length, stepping up after each round.

Circular
Circular peyote is worked in continuous rounds like tubular peyote, but the rounds stay flat and radiate outward from the center as a result of increasing the number of beads per stitch or using larger beads. If the number or size of the beads is not sufficient to fill the spaces between stitches, the circle will not lie flat.

Zipping up or joining
To join two sections of a flat peyote piece invisibly, match up the two pieces so the end rows fit together. "Zip up" the pieces by zigzagging through the up-beads on both ends.

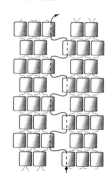

Square stitch
[1] String all the beads needed for the first row, and then pick wup the first bead of the second row. Sew though the last bead of the first row and the first bead of the second row again. Position the two beads side by side so that their holes are parallel.

[2] Pick up the next bead of row 2, and sew through the corresponding bead in row 1 and the new bead in row 1. Repeat across the row.

STRINGING & WIREWORK

Crimping

Use crimp beads to secure flexible beading wire. Slide the crimp bead into place, and squeeze it firmly with chainnose pliers to flatten it. For a more finished look, use crimping pliers.

[1] Position the crimp bead in the hole that is closest to the handle of the crimping pliers.

[2] Holding the wires apart, squeeze the pliers to compress the crimp bead, making sure one wire is on each side of the dent.

[3] Place the crimp bead in the front hole of the pliers, and position it so the dent is facing the tips of the pliers. Squeeze the pliers to fold the crimp in half.

Opening and closing loops and jump rings

[1] Hold a loop or a jump ring with two pairs of pliers, such as chainnose, flatnose, or bentnose pliers.

[2] To open the loop or jump ring, bring the tips of one pair of pliers toward you, and push the tips of the other pair away from you. Reverse the steps to close.

Plain loop

[1] Using chainnose pliers, make a right-angle bend in the wire directly above a bead or other component or at least ¼ in. (6 mm) from the end of a piece of wire. For a larger loop, bend the wire further in.

[2] Grasp the end of the wire with roundnose pliers so that the wire is flush with the jaws of the pliers where they meet. The closer to the tip of the pliers that you work, the smaller the loop will be. Press downward slightly, and rotate the wire toward the bend made in step 1.

[3] Reposition the pliers in the loop to continue rotating the wire until the end of the wire touches the bend.

Wraps above a top-drilled bead

[1] Center a top-drilled bead on a 3-in. (7.6 cm) piece of wire. Bend each wire end upward, crossing them into an X above the bead.

[2] Using chainnose pliers, make a small bend in each wire end to form a right angle where the wires cross.

[3] Wrap the horizontal wire around the vertical wire as in a wrapped loop (see "Wrapped loop"). Trim the excess wrapping wire.

[4] If desired, make a wrapped loop (see "Wrapped loop") with the vertical wire directly above the wraps.

Wrapped loop

[1] Using chainnose pliers, make a right-angle bend in the wire about 2 mm above a bead or other component or at least 1¼ in. (3.2 cm) from the end of a piece of wire.

[2] Position the jaws of the roundnose pliers in the bend. The closer to the tip of the pliers that you work, the smaller the loop will be.

[3] Curve the short end of the wire over the top jaw of the roundnose pliers.

[4] Reposition the pliers so the lower jaw fits snugly in the loop. Curve the wire downward around the bottom jaw of the pliers. This is the first half of a wrapped loop.

[5] To complete the wraps, grasp the top of the loop with one pair of pliers.

[6] With another pair of pliers, wrap the wire around the stem two or three times. Trim the excess wire, and gently press the cut end close to the wraps with chainnose pliers.

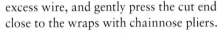

Necklace Fitting 101

Find the perfect length for your designs to complement the people who wear them

by **Maggie Roschyk**

In an ideal world, selecting and wearing jewelry would be straightforward: You see the necklace, you love the necklace, you buy the necklace, you wear the necklace.

But realistically, many consumers buy beautiful handcrafted jewelry — especially necklaces — that they hardly ever wear. Let's be honest with ourselves and ask, "Why aren't we wearing these pieces?" The answer may have to do with the way a necklace fits.

Know your necklace lengths

Commercial fashion designers create clothing that fits a range of sizes. That's smart, to say the least. Jewelry designers, on the other hand, often make one-sized pieces that typically fit whoever created them.

Think about the dynamics of these two approaches. Form often takes over during the creation process, and function is left on the side of the road. But when you create something, don't you want it to be worn and enjoyed? And when you buy a gorgeous necklace, wouldn't it be nice if you could actually wear it?

So let's focus on function for a moment, beginning with industry guidelines for necklace lengths.

- *Choker and collar length*, 13–16 in. (33–41 cm): Chokers and collars lie on the neck or just above the collarbone. Making a necklace this length can be tricky. Some people love and look attractive in chokers, others do not. Also, a collarbone-length piece needs to be measured on

each person — there's not much room for error. Including an extender chain on the piece helps ensure a comfortable fit.
- *Princess length*, 17–19 in. (43–48 cm): Princess-length necklaces fall just below the collarbone. This is probably the most common necklace length. Keep in mind that if the necklace hangs too low, it can bounce around on the chest and slip under clothing, hidden from view.
- *Matinee length*, 20–24 in. (51–61 cm): This length necklace drapes onto the chest. It is a very modern and trendy length and is perfect for necklaces featuring large focals.
- *Opera length*, 28–32 in. (71–81 cm): Opera-length pieces drape onto the mid-section of the body. This is a wonderful length, especially if the beads have a texture that the wearer will want to touch. Be mindful of using materials that could break. This length can swing and smack into a car door, so avoid focals that will flap around. Also, this length requires a special focus on balance. Remember that the heaviest part of your necklace will answer the call of gravity and shift downward.
- *Lariats and ropes*, more than 40 in. (1 m): Long necklaces are the multitaskers of jewelry. Wrap them around your neck once, twice, even three times. Lariats and ropes are versatile and can work with any neckline.

Choker and collar length, 13–16 in. (33–41 cm)

Princess length, 17–19 in. (43–48 cm)

Matinee length, 20–24 in. (51–61 cm)

Real fit for real bodies

Industry guidelines can be very useful when making jewelry. They prevent us from creating pieces that are 10 in. (25 cm) long — generally too long for a bracelet and too short for a necklace. They also help us understand how a designer intended a piece to fit.

But guidelines alone are not enough. We need to take into consideration the different sizes and shapes of people and their preferences for how things fit. Designing jewelry for yourself and others must involve some custom tailoring. Remember, haute couture is custom fitted and impeccably tailored. Why not do the same for your one-of-a-kind creations?

Here are six tips for customizing your designs to fit the intended wearer.

1 Purchase a yard of heavy cotton cord, available from any craft or fabric store. Tape the ends to prevent unraveling. When determining the perfect necklace length, drape the cotton cord around the wearer's neck. You can mark the length on the cord with a marker and use a tape measure to record that measurement. Why use cotton cord? The cord will drape, whereas beading wire or thread will not.

2 You can also use the industry guidelines to determine the perfect length. Take these descriptions of necklace lengths to the wearer and see how they match the body you're fitting. For most industry guidelines, there is a range in length. Which length in a range suits the wearer?

Also, neck diameter differs from person to person, which changes where a necklace will fall on the body when worn. Does 17 in. (43 cm) actually fall just below the collarbone on the wearer? If not, figure out how much you need to adjust.

3 If the wearer likes the fit of a favorite necklace, measure it and use that measurement as a guideline when making her custom piece.

4 When making projects from this book, use the measurement listed in the materials list as a guideline. If you are making an 18-in. (46 cm) necklace, you know the designer intended it to sit just below the collarbone. Follow tip 1, 2, or 3 to determine if you need to change the length.

5 If you are using a focal bead, where will it fall in relation to the décolleté? A large focal can fall into cleavage or disappear under the neckline of clothing — not attractive. Large focals work best in necklaces that fall between princess and matinee length, or between matinee and opera length. These lengths position the focal safely above or below the bustline.

6 Ignore suggestions that small people should only wear dainty jewelry or large people should wear larger pieces. If you love it and feel comfortable in it, wear it. Use industry standards only as a guideline for where a necklace is expected to fall.

Custom-tailored necklaces possess a tangible worth to the wearer. A woman appreciates it when jewelry is made for her body. Plus, you feel great knowing that you've created jewelry that's both attractive and will be worn comfortably. How haute couture is that?

Opera length, 28–32 in. (71–81 cm)

Lariats and ropes, more than 40 in. (1 m)

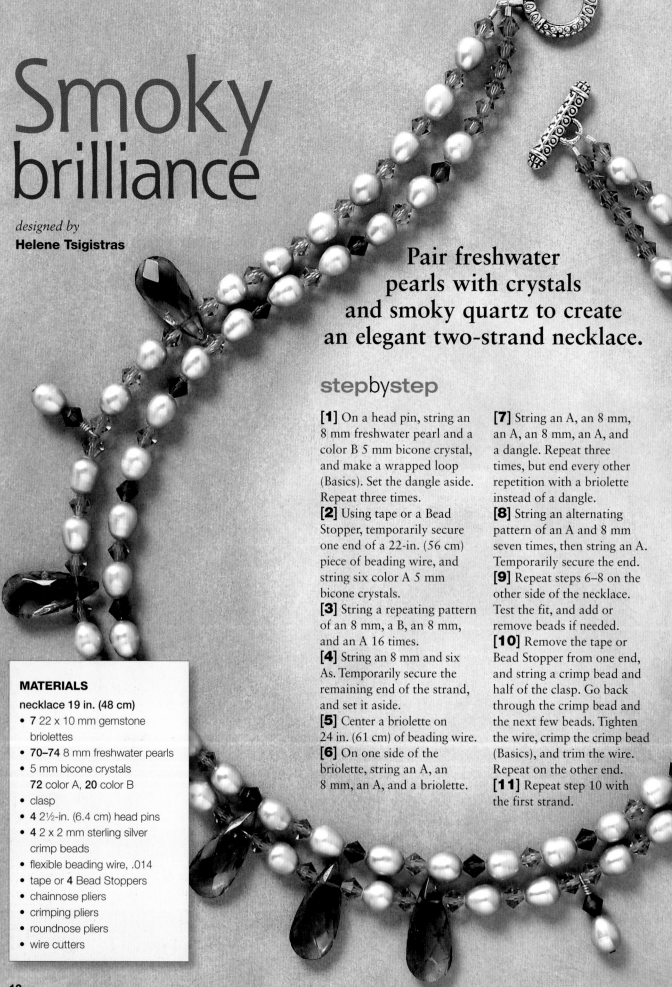

Smoky brilliance

designed by
Helene Tsigistras

**Pair freshwater
pearls with crystals
and smoky quartz to create
an elegant two-strand necklace.**

stepbystep

[1] On a head pin, string an 8 mm freshwater pearl and a color B 5 mm bicone crystal, and make a wrapped loop (Basics). Set the dangle aside. Repeat three times.

[2] Using tape or a Bead Stopper, temporarily secure one end of a 22-in. (56 cm) piece of beading wire, and string six color A 5 mm bicone crystals.

[3] String a repeating pattern of an 8 mm, a B, an 8 mm, and an A 16 times.

[4] String an 8 mm and six As. Temporarily secure the remaining end of the strand, and set it aside.

[5] Center a briolette on 24 in. (61 cm) of beading wire.

[6] On one side of the briolette, string an A, an 8 mm, an A, and a briolette.

[7] String an A, an 8 mm, an A, an 8 mm, an A, and a dangle. Repeat three times, but end every other repetition with a briolette instead of a dangle.

[8] String an alternating pattern of an A and 8 mm seven times, then string an A. Temporarily secure the end.

[9] Repeat steps 6–8 on the other side of the necklace. Test the fit, and add or remove beads if needed.

[10] Remove the tape or Bead Stopper from one end, and string a crimp bead and half of the clasp. Go back through the crimp bead and the next few beads. Tighten the wire, crimp the crimp bead (Basics), and trim the wire. Repeat on the other end.

[11] Repeat step 10 with the first strand.

MATERIALS

necklace 19 in. (48 cm)
- **7** 22 x 10 mm gemstone briolettes
- **70–74** 8 mm freshwater pearls
- 5 mm bicone crystals
  72 color A, **20 color B**
- clasp
- **4** 2½-in. (6.4 cm) head pins
- **4** 2 x 2 mm sterling silver crimp beads
- flexible beading wire, .014
- tape or **4** Bead Stoppers
- chainnose pliers
- crimping pliers
- roundnose pliers
- wire cutters

Glass garland

Combine different shapes and colors of Czech glass beads for a bountiful necklace

designed by **Lesley Weiss**

stepbystep

[1] Cut a 21-in. (53 cm) piece of beading wire. String a crimp bead and one loop of half of the clasp. Go back through the crimp bead, and crimp it (Basics).

[2] String a 4 mm fire-polished bead, an 8 mm rondelle, and 16 in. (41 cm) of assorted Czech glass beads interspersed with 4 mms and 8 mms. End with an 8 mm and a 4 mm, and secure the strand with a Bead Stopper.

[3] Cut a 26-in. (66 cm) piece of beading wire, and string a crimp bead and the other loop of half of the clasp. Go back through the crimp bead, and crimp it.

[4] String a 4 mm and 20 in. (51 cm) of Czech glass beads, interspersed with 8 mms. End with a 4 mm, and secure the end with a Bead Stopper.

[5] Twist the long strand around the short strand until they are the same length, distributing the twist evenly. Test the fit, and add or remove beads as needed.

[6] Remove the Bead Stopper from the end of a strand, and string a crimp bead and a loop of the other half of the clasp, taking care to attach it to the appropriate loop. Go back through the crimp bead, and crimp it. Repeat with the other strand.

MATERIALS

necklace 16½ in. (41.9 cm)

- **3 or more** 8-in. (20 cm) strands of Czech glass beads in a variety of colors and shapes, including daggers, petals, and paddles
- 8-in. (20 cm) strand 8 mm glass rondelles
- 4-in. (10 cm) strand 4 mm fire-polished beads
- 2-strand clasp
- 4 crimp beads
- flexible beading wire, .014
- 2 Bead Stoppers
- crimping pliers
- wire cutters

Asymmetrical amethyst

Pair your favorite metal and gemstone in a swingy multistrand

designed by **Stacy Werkheiser**

stepbystep

[1] Cut a 2½-in. (6.4 cm) piece of 22-gauge wire, and make the first half of a wrapped loop (Basics). String a 6–7 mm round bead, and make the first half of a wrapped loop. Make eight bead units.

[2] Attach one loop of a bead unit to a 30–32 mm hammered ring, and complete the wraps. Attach the other loop to the end of a 12-in. (30 cm) piece of small-link chain, and complete the wraps. Open a 7–8 mm jump ring (Basics), and attach the other end of the chain to another hammered ring. Close the jump ring.

[3] Arrange the bead units along the chain as desired. For each bead unit, cut and remove a chain link, attach the loops of the unit to the unattached chain links, and complete the wraps.

[4] Cut an 18-in. (46 cm) piece of beading wire. Center 13 in. (33 cm) of 10–12 mm round beads and 5–6 mm spacers. On each end of the wire, string a crimp bead and a hammered ring. Go back through the crimp bead and the last few beads on each end, crimp the crimp beads (Basics), and trim the excess wire.

[5] Cut a 3-in. (7.6 cm) piece of wire, and make the first half of a wrapped loop. String a spacer, a 10–12 mm round, and a spacer. Make the first half of a wrapped loop. Make seven 10–12 mm bead units.

[6] Cut an 18-in. (46 cm) piece of large-link chain, and repeat step 3. Use jump rings to attach each end of the chain and a hammered ring.

[7] On a head pin, string a spacer, a 10–12 mm round, and a spacer, and make the first half of a wrapped loop. Attach the jump ring from step 2, and complete the wraps.

MATERIALS

necklace 38 in. (97 cm)

- **2** 8-in. (20 cm) strands 10–12 mm round beads
- **8** 6–7 mm round beads
- **36–46** 5–6 mm spacers
- **2** 30–32 mm hammered rings
- 41 in. (1 m) 22-gauge wire, half-hard
- 18 in. (46 cm) chain, 20–22 mm (large) links
- 12 in. (30 cm) chain, 5–6 mm (small) links
- 2-in. (5 cm) head pin
- **3** 7–8 mm jump rings
- **2** crimp beads
- flexible beading wire, .014–.015
- chainnose pliers
- crimping pliers
- roundnose pliers
- wire cutters

Rock collector

Capture the eye of an aspiring geologist with pyrite chunks, lava lentils, and blue goldstone

designed by **Tea Benduhn**

stepbystep

[1] On a 2-in. (5 cm) head pin, string the largest of the 10–15 mm pyrite nuggets. Make a plain loop (Basics) at the end of the head pin.

[2] Repeat step 1 twice on two 1½-in. (3.8 cm) head pins using the remaining pyrite nuggets.

[3] Cut an 18-in. (46 cm) piece of beading wire. String a crimp bead and half of the clasp. Go back through the crimp bead, and crimp it (Basics).

[4] Over both ends of wire, string 4 x 6 mm faceted blue goldstone beads until the short end of the wire is covered. Over the remaining wire, continue stringing 4 x 6 mms for a total of 25.

[5] String three 18–20 mm lentil beads, the loop of a 1½-in. (3.8 cm) head pin, a lentil, the loop of the 2-in. (5 cm) head pin, a lentil, the loop of a 1½-in. (3.8 cm) head pin, three lentils, and 25 4 x 6 mms.

[6] String a crimp bead and the remaining half of the clasp. Go back through the crimp bead and a few 4 x 6 mms. Crimp the crimp bead, and trim the excess wire.

[7] Using crimping pliers, close crimp covers over the crimps.

MATERIALS

necklace 15 in. (38 cm)

- 8 18–20 mm lava lentil beads (Fire Mountain Gems and Beads, firemountaingems.com)
- 3 10–15 mm pyrite nuggets (Fire Mountain Gems and Beads)
- 50 4 x 6 mm faceted blue goldstone beads
- clasp
- 2-in. (5 cm) head pin
- 2 1½-in. (3.8 cm) head pins
- 2 crimp beads
- 2 crimp covers
- flexible beading wire, .018
- chainnose pliers
- crimping pliers
- roundnose pliers
- wire cutters

On track

Different sized beads shape a wearable railroad

designed by **Lynne Soto**

MATERIALS

necklace 18 in. (46 cm)
- **80** 15 mm Czech glass two-hole spacer bars (Bead Knots, beadknots.com)
- **83** 5 mm silver-plate melon beads (New Mexico Bead and Fetish, nmbeadandfetish.com)
- **2** 5 mm silver-plate round beads (New Mexico Bead and Fetish)
- **83** 2.4 mm silver-plate round beads (New Mexico Bead and Fetish)
- clasp
- **2** crimp beads
- flexible beading wire, .014
- **4** Bead Stoppers
- crimping pliers
- wire cutters

stepbystep

[1] Cut two 24-in. (61 cm) pieces of beading wire, and attach a Bead Stopper 4 in. (10 cm) from one end of each wire.

[2] On one wire, string one hole of a two-hole spacer bar and a 2.4 mm round bead. Repeat six times.

[3] String a spacer bar and a 5 mm melon bead. Repeat four times.

[4] Repeat steps 2 and 3 five times.

[5] Repeat step 2, but pick up eight pairs of beads, omitting the last 2.4 mm. Attach a Bead Stopper after the last bead.

[6] With the other wire, go through the remaining hole of the first spacer bar, and string a melon bead.

Continue stringing a bead between each spacer bar that is different than the one on the other strand. Do not pick up a bead after the last spacer. Snug up the beads to form an undulating curve (**photo a**), and attach a Bead Stopper.

[7] Working with one end of the necklace at a time, remove the Bead Stoppers and string a 2.4 mm bead and a melon bead on each wire. Over both wires, string a crimp bead, a 5 mm round bead, and half the clasp. With both wires, go back through the 5 mm bead and the crimp bead. Snug up the beads, crimp the crimp bead (Basics and **photo b**), and trim the excess wire. Repeat on the other end.

Regal
presentation

**Create visual impact
with symmetry and
contrasting materials**

designed by **Mark Avery**

Beaded beads are the focal point of this strung necklace. The availability of a variety of faceted and round gemstones widens your color options. Let this necklace inspire your own version.

stepbystep

Beaded beads

You will be working with two lengths of thread. These will be referred to as thread #1 and #2. At the start of each step, the instructions will tell you which needle to use.

[1] Thread a needle on each end of 24 in. (61 cm) of thread, and center six 5 mm spacers. Cross one of the needles through an end spacer to form a ring. This is thread #1.

FIGURE 1

[2] Cut a second 24-in. (61 cm) length of thread, thread a needle on each end, and sew through all the spacers, starting with the spacer opposite where thread #1 exits **(figure 1)**. This is thread #2. Position the ring with thread #1 facing the top.

[3] On thread #1, with the left-hand needle, pick up two 4 mm gemstone beads, a spacer, and two 4 mms. With the right-hand needle, cross through the last 4 mm picked up **(figure 2, a–b and e–f)**.

[4] With the left-hand needle, pick up a 4 mm, a spacer, and two 4 mms. With the right-hand needle, sew through the next spacer in the ring, and cross

MATERIALS

necklace 23½ in. (59.7 cm)

- 16 mm faceted round glass bead
- **2** 12 mm faceted round glass beads
- **14** 12 x 8 mm faceted gemstone beads
- **16** 8–10 mm Bali vermeil beads
- **42** 6 mm round gemstone beads
- **108** 4 mm round gemstone beads
- **24** 5 mm Bali vermeil spacers
- **48** 4 mm Bali vermeil spacers
- clasp
- 2 crimp beads
- bonded nylon thread, color to match beads
- flexible beading wire, .018–.024
- beading needles, #12
- crimping pliers
- wire cutters

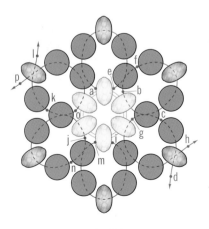

FIGURE 2

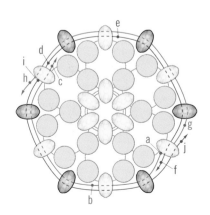

FIGURE 3

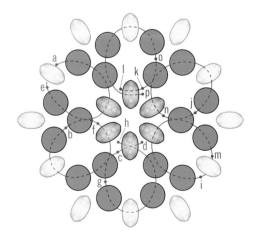

FIGURE 4

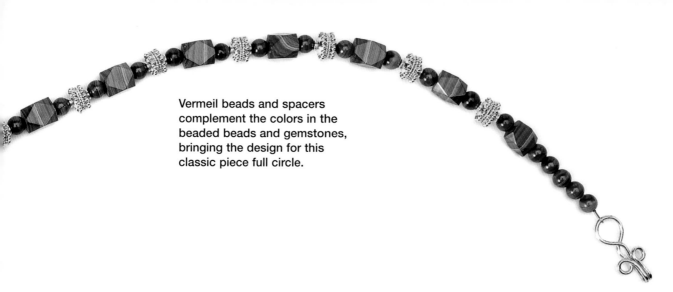

Vermeil beads and spacers complement the colors in the beaded beads and gemstones, bringing the design for this classic piece full circle.

through the last 4 mm picked up (b–c and f–g).

[5] With the left-hand needle, pick up a 4 mm and a spacer. With the right-hand needle, sew through the next spacer in the ring, pick up two 4 mms, and cross through the last spacer picked up (c–d and g–h).

[6] On thread #2, with the left-hand needle, sew through the first 4 mm picked up with the right-hand needle in step 5, and pick up a 4 mm, a spacer, and two 4 mms. With the right-hand needle, cross through the last 4 mm picked up (i–j and m–n).

[7] With the left-hand needle, pick up a 4 mm, a spacer, and two 4 mms. With the right-hand needle, sew through the next spacer in the ring, and cross through the last 4 mm picked up (j–k and n–o).

[8] With the left-hand needle, pick up a 4 mm and a spacer. With the right-hand needle, sew through the next spacer in the ring and the first 4 mm picked up in step 3. Pick up a 4 mm, and cross through the last spacer picked up (k–l and o–p).

[9] With a needle from thread #1, pick up a spacer, and sew through the next spacer (figure 3, a–b). Repeat twice (b–c). With a needle from thread #2, working in the same direction, pick up a spacer, and sew through the next spacer (d–e). Repeat twice (e–f). With a thread that was not used to pick up a spacer, sew in the opposite direction through six spacers (g–h). Repeat with the other thread that was not used to pick up spacers (i–j). Snug up the spacers.

[10] Insert the 16 mm bead into the beadwork.

[11] To form the other half of the beaded bead, on thread #1, with the left-hand needle, pick up two 4 mms, a spacer, and a 4 mm. With the right-hand needle, pick up a 4 mm, and cross through the last 4 mm picked up with the left-hand needle (figure 4, a–b and e–f).

[12] With the left-hand needle, pick up a spacer and a 4 mm. With the right-hand needle, pick up a 4 mm, skip a spacer in the middle ring, sew through the next spacer, pick up a 4 mm, and cross through the last 4 mm picked up with the left-hand needle (b–c and f–g).

[13] With the left-hand needle, pick up a spacer. With the right-hand needle, pick up a 4 mm, skip a spacer, and sew through the next spacer in the middle ring. Pick up two 4 mms, and cross through the spacer just added (c–d and g–h).

[14] On thread #2, with the left-hand needle, pick up a 4 mm, and sew through the adjacent 4 mm of the previous stitch. Pick up a spacer and a 4 mm. With the right-hand needle, pick up a 4 mm, and cross through the last 4 mm picked up with the left-hand needle (i–j and m–n).

[15] With the left-hand needle, pick up a spacer and a 4 mm. With the right-hand needle, pick up a 4 mm, skip a spacer in the middle ring, sew through the next spacer, pick up a 4 mm, and

cross through the last 4 mm picked up with the left-hand needle (j–k and n–o).

[16] With the left-hand needle, pick up a spacer. With the right-hand needle, pick up a 4 mm, skip a spacer, and sew through the next spacer in the middle ring. Pick up a 4 mm, sew through the adjacent 4 mm in the first stitch, and cross through the spacer picked up in this step (k–l and o–p).

[17] Sew through the end ring of spacers with each of the threads. End the threads (Basics).

[18] Repeat steps 1–17 to make two more beads, but use 4 mm spacers instead of 5 mms and a 12 mm bead in step 10 instead of a 16 mm.

Necklace

[1] Cut a 30-in. (76 cm) piece of beading wire, and center the largest beaded bead.

[2] On each end, string a 6 mm gemstone bead, an 8–10 mm Bali bead, a 6 mm, and a beaded bead.

[3] On each end, string a 6 mm, an 8–10 mm, a 6 mm, and a 12 x 8 mm faceted gemstone bead. Repeat six times.

[4] On each end, string five 6 mms, a crimp bead, and half of the clasp. Go back through the crimp beads and two or three beads, crimp the crimp beads (Basics), and trim the tails.

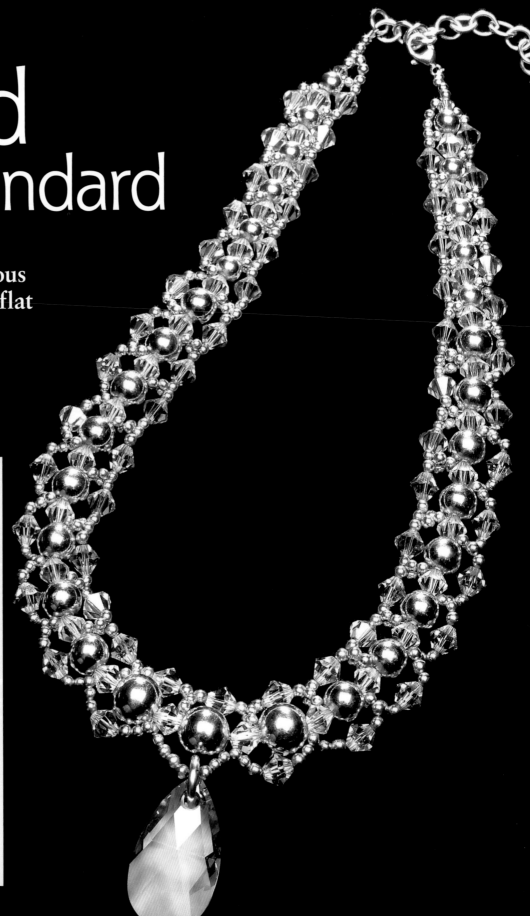

The gold standard

Create a gorgeous necklace using flat spiral stitch

designed by **April Bradley**

MATERIALS

necklace 17 in. (43 cm)

- 1⅛ x ¹¹⁄₁₆-in. (2.9 x 1.7 cm) crystal pendant
- round beads
  3 10 mm
  16 8 mm
  12 6 mm
  132 3 mm
  192 2 mm
- bicone crystals
  86 6 mm
  2 4 mm
- clasp
- 8 mm jump ring
- **2** crimp beads
- **2** crimp covers (optional)
- Fireline 8 lb. test
- flexible beading wire, .014
- beading needles, #12
- Bead Stopper or tape (optional)
- **2** pairs of chainnose pliers
- crimping pliers
- wire cutters

As a variation, substitute 13 x 6.5 mm crystal pendants in place of five 6 mm bicones along every other bottom loop of the necklace.

Adorn your neckline with sparkling crystals and bright gold beads in a necklace that works up so quickly, you'll be able to make it the evening before an evening out.

stepbystep

Base row

[1] On 24 in. (61 cm) of beading wire, string a crimp bead and half of the clasp 2 in. (5 cm) from one end. Go back through the crimp bead, and crimp it (Basics). Trim the short tail.

[2] String four 3 mm round beads, a 4 mm bicone crystal, a repeating pattern of a 6 mm round bead and a 6 mm bicone crystal six times, a repeating pattern of an 8 mm round bead and a 6 mm bicone eight times, a repeating pattern of a 10 mm round bead and a 6 mm bicone three times, a repeating pattern of an 8 mm round and a 6 mm bicone eight times, a repeating pattern of a 6 mm round and a 6 mm bicone six times, a 6 mm round, a 4 mm bicone, and four 3 mm rounds.

[3] String a crimp bead and the other half of the clasp, and go back through the crimp bead. Leaving about 4 mm of space between the last bead strung and the crimp bead, crimp the crimp bead. Or, temporarily secure this end with a Bead Stopper or tape until you finish the necklace.

Spiral loops

[1] On 2 yd. (1.8 m) of Fireline, attach a stop bead (Basics), leaving a 6-in. (15 cm) tail. Sew through the first 6 mm round and 6 mm bicone on the base.

[2] Pick up a 2 mm round bead, a 3 mm round, a 6 mm bicone, a 3 mm round, and a 2 mm round. Sew through the first 6 mm round and bicone again, and continue through the next 6 mm round.

Push the loop to the right of the base (figure 1).

[3] Repeat step 2, but sew through the bicone and the round your thread exited at the start of this step, and continue through the next bicone. Push the loop to the left (figure 2).

[4] Repeat steps 2 and 3 for a total of eight loops, pushing the loops to alternate sides and always sewing through the two beads your thread exited at the start of the step and the next bead in the base.

[5] Continue making loops, but instead of picking up one 2 mm round, pick up two. Make a total of 19 loops.

[6] Make one loop using two 2 mm rounds, four 3 mm rounds, and two 2 mm rounds.

[7] Make 19 loops as in step 5, and eight loops as in step 4. End the working thread and tail (Basics).

[8] Lay the necklace out on your work surface, making sure the first loop lies to the right of the base, and the next loop lies to the left of the base. The center loop of round beads only defines the outer center loop of the necklace.

[9] On 1 yd. (.9 m) of Fireline, attach a stop bead, leaving a 6-in. (15 cm) tail. Sew through the first 3 mm round, 6 mm bicone, and 3 mm round in the first loop of the inner edge.

[10] Sew through the 3 mm round, 6 mm bicone, and 3 mm round in the next loop along the inner edge (figure 3). Repeat until you reach the last inner loop.

[11] Pulling gently, snug up the inner edge into a curve that sits comfortably around your neck.

[12] Pick up three 3 mm rounds, and sew into the 3 mm round and the 4 mm bicone on the base. End the working thread. Remove the stop bead, and repeat with the tail.

[13] Open an 8 mm jump ring (Basics), and attach the pendant to the center outer loop of round beads. Close the jump ring.

[14] Use chainnose pliers to close crimp covers over the crimp beads if desired.

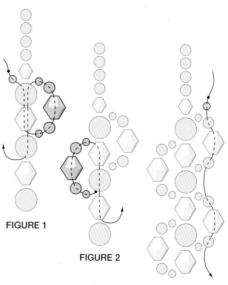

FIGURE 1

FIGURE 2

FIGURE 3

Peacock fan

**Bright colors make a
bold statement in this
fanciful piece**

designed by **Jenny Van**

a

b

c

d

e

f

MATERIALS

necklace 19 in. (48 cm)

- 4 mm bicone crystals
  70 color A
  76 color B
- 4 mm round or bicone
  crystal, color C
- **76** 3 mm bicone crystals,
  color D
- **20** 3 mm round crystals,
  color C
- 4–5 g 15º seed beads
- curved bar links (sold as
  chain, jjbead.com)
  2 14 mm
  38 9 mm
  38 7 mm
- clasp
- **2** 4 mm jump rings
- Fireline 6 or 8 lb. test
- beading needles, #12
- **2** pairs of pliers
- wire cutters

SINGLE STITCHES

stepbystep

Curved bar links are often
sold as chain. Cut apart the
chain links before beginning.

Necklace

[1] Thread a needle on each
end of 4 ft. (1.2 m) of Fireline. Center a color C 4 mm
round or bicone crystal, a
15º seed bead, a color A
4 mm bicone crystal, a 15º,
an A, a 15º, an A, and a 15º.
Sew through the C 4 mm to
form a ring (photo a).
[2] With one needle, pick up
a 14 mm link, a 9 mm link,
a 7 mm link, a 15º, a color D
3 mm bicone crystal, a 15º,

a D, and a 15º. Sew through
the remaining hole of the
7 mm link (photo b). Pick up
a 15º, a color B 4 mm bicone
crystal, and a 15º. Sew
through the remaining hole
of the 9 mm link (photo c).
Pick up a 15º, an A, and a
15º, and sew through the
remaining hole of the 14 mm
link (photo d). Repeat this
step with the other needle.
[3] With one needle, pick up
a 15º, a B, a 15º, an A, a 15º,
a B, and a 15º, and sew
through the next 14 mm link,
15º, and A (photo e). With
the other needle, sew through
the beadwork to exit the same
A in the opposite direction.

[4] With one needle, pick up
a 15º, an A, and a 15º. Repeat
with the other needle. With
one needle, pick up a color C
3 mm round crystal, and
cross the other needle
through it (photo f).
[5] With one needle, pick up
a 9 mm link, a 7 mm link, a
15º, a D, a 15º, a D, and a
15º, and sew through the
remaining hole of the 7 mm
link (photo g). Pick up a 15º,
a B, and a 15º, and sew
through the remaining hole
of the 9 mm link (photo h).
Pick up a 15º and a B.
Repeat the entire step with
the other needle.

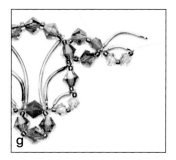

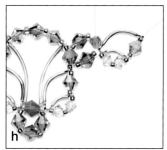

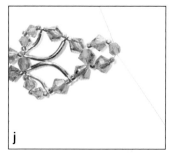

[6] With one needle, pick up an A, and cross the other needle through it (photo i).

[7] Repeat steps 4 (photo j), 5, and 6 until you have a total of nine units on one side of the necklace.

[8] With one needle, pick up a 15º, an A, and a 15º. Repeat with the other needle. With one needle, pick up a C 3 mm, and cross the other needle through it. With one needle, pick up a 15º, an A, and a 15º. Repeat with the other needle. With one needle, pick up an A, and cross the other needle through it. With one needle, pick up 10 15ºs, and cross the other needle through them. Retrace the thread

path through the 15ºs to reinforce the loop, retrace the thread path through the last few units, and end the threads (Basics).

[9] Thread a needle on each end of 4 ft. (1.2 m) of Fireline, and center it in the side A opposite the first half of the necklace. Repeat steps 4–8 to complete the second side of the necklace.

[10] Open a jump ring (Basics), attach half of the clasp and a loop of 15ºs on one end of the necklace, and close the jump ring. Repeat on the other end.

Through &through

Layers of interlocked scallops create a beautiful collar

designed by **Kara Jacob**

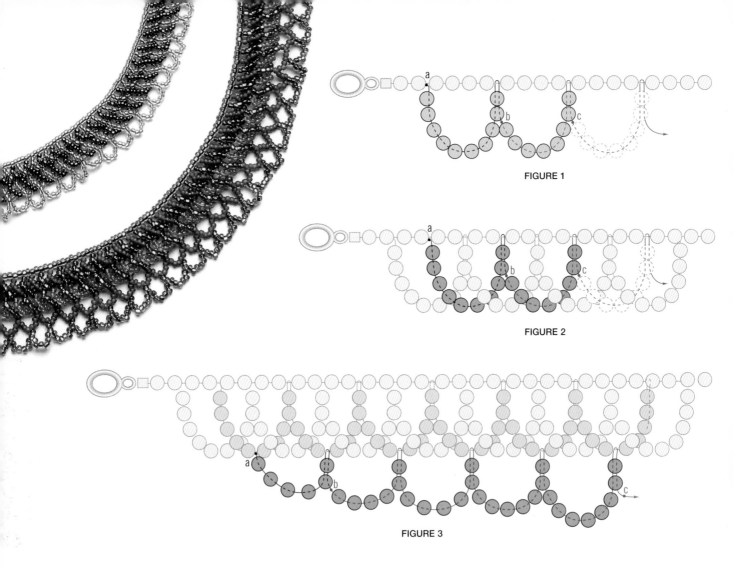

FIGURE 1

FIGURE 2

FIGURE 3

This layered, modified, scalloped netting stitch comes from the Xhosa tribe of South Africa. With the addition of single scallop layers, the necklace has a lacy, feminine feel.

stepbystep

[1] Determine the desired finished length of your necklace, add 6 in. (15 cm), and cut a piece of beading wire to that length. At one end of the wire, string a crimp bead and the lobster claw clasp. Go back through the crimp bead, and crimp it (Basics).

[2] String enough color A 11º seed beads to reach your desired necklace length, and secure the end of the beading wire with a Bead Stopper.

[3] On a comfortable length of thread, attach a stop bead (Basics), leaving a 6-in. (15 cm) tail, and sew through a few As on the base to exit two As from the clasp. Pick up 10 As, and snug them up to the wire. Skip four As on the base, and sew under the wire, over the wire, and back through the last two As **(figure 1, a–b)**. Pick up eight As, skip four As on the base, sew under and over the wire, and sew back through the last two As **(b–c)**. Continue adding netted scallops until you reach the other end of the necklace. Remove the stop bead, and end the working thread and tail (Basics).

[4] On a comfortable length of thread, attach a stop bead, leaving a 6-in. (15 cm) tail, and sew through a few As on the base to exit four As from the clasp. Pick up 10 color B 11º seed beads, holding them in front of the clasp. Pick up 10 As, and snug them up to the wire. Skip four As on the base, and sew under the wire, over the wire, and back through the last two As **(figure 1, a–b)**. Pick up eight As, skip four As on the base, sew under and over the wire, and sew back through the last two As **(b–c)**. Continue adding netted scallops until you reach the other end of the necklace. Remove the stop bead, and end the working thread and tail (Basics).

As, and snug them up to the wire. Bring the Bs under the next loop of As, skip four As on the base, and sew under and over the wire, and back through the last two Bs **(figure 2, a–b)**.

[5] Bring the thread in front of the As, pick up eight Bs, and bring them under the next loop of As. Skip four As on the base, and sew under and over the wire, and back through the last two Bs **(b–c)**. Repeat to the end of the base, remove the stop bead, and end the working thread and tail.

[6] On a comfortable length of thread, attach a stop bead, leaving a 6-in. (15 cm) tail, and sew through a few Bs to exit the center of the first loop of Bs. Pick up six Bs, and sew under and over the thread in the center of the next loop of Bs, and back through the last two Bs added **(figure 3, a–b)**. Repeat four times, increasing the number of Bs in each stitch by one until you are picking up

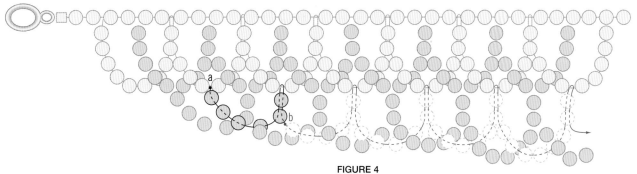

FIGURE 4

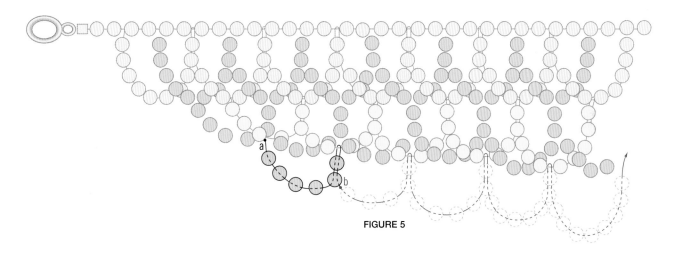

FIGURE 5

eight Bs per stitch (b–c). Continue adding netted scallops until you have four stitches left, and then decrease the number of beads in each stitch to mirror the other end of the necklace. Remove the stop bead, and end the working thread and tail.

[7] On a comfortable length of thread, attach a stop bead, leaving a 6-in. (15 cm) tail, and sew through a few As to exit the center of the second loop of As, in front of the beadwork. Pick up six color C 11º seed beads, bring the Cs behind the loop of Bs, and sew under and over the thread in the center of the next loop of As, and back through the last two Cs (figure 4, a–b). Bring the thread in front of the beadwork, and begin making a second layer of scallop stitches, as in step 5, sewing around the thread in the center of each scallop of As from the row before, and increasing the number of Cs in each stitch by one

until you are picking up eight. Continue until you are four stitches from the end, and then decrease the number of beads in each stitch to mirror the other end of the necklace. Remove the stop bead, and end the working thread and tail.

[8] Repeat step 6 with Bs or Cs to add a single layer of netted scallops to the bottom of the second row (figure 5). Repeat step 6 once more with a different color, to add a final row of single-layer netted scallops.

[9] Remove the Bead Stopper, and string a crimp bead and the soldered jump ring. Go back through the crimp bead, crimp, and trim the tail.

MATERIALS

necklace 23 in. (58 cm)

- 9–12 g 11º seed beads, in each of **3** colors: A, B, C
- lobster claw clasp and soldered jump ring
- **2** crimp beads
- flexible beading wire, .010–.014
- nylon beading thread, size D
- beading needles, #12 or #13
- Bead Stopper
- crimping pliers
- wire cutters

Loop
de loop

Loopy beaded beads light up lampworked glass in this necklace

designed by **Jessica Fehrmann**

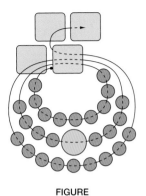

FIGURE

a

b

Embellish peyote tubes with loops to complement lampworked beads. Attach drop beads to chain to complete the textured look.

stepbystep

Beaded beads

[1] On a comfortable length of Fireline, attach a stop bead (Basics), leaving a 6-in. (15 cm) tail. Working in even-count peyote stitch (Basics), use 11º cylinder beads to make a strip that is two beads wide and eight rows long with four beads on each straight edge. Zip up (Basics) the ends of the strip to form a tube, and do not end the threads. String the tube on a short piece of beading wire as you work the next step. This will help you locate the opening of the tube later.

[2] Exiting a cylinder in the tube, pick up nine 15ºs. Sew through the same cylinder in the tube to create a loop. Pick up four 15º seed beads, a 6º seed bead, and four 15ºs, and sew through the same cylinder in the tube. Make a third loop using nine 15ºs **(figure)**.

[3] Sew through an adjacent cylinder in the tube, and repeat step 2. Repeat around the tube to add three loops around each cylinder. For a more random look, change the location of the 6º in each loop. Occasionally substitute a drop bead for the 6º. Remove the stop bead, and end the threads (Basics).

[4] Repeat steps 1–3 for a total of eight beaded beads.

Strung centerpiece

[1] Cut a 10-in. (25 cm) piece of beading wire, and string a 6º, a beaded bead, a 6º, a bead aligner (flat side first), a lampworked bead, and a bead aligner (pointed side first). Repeat the pattern

DESIGN NOTE:
You can purchase 4.5 mm jump rings for the drop beads and 5.5 mm jump rings for the 6º beads if you do not want to make your own. Add or omit jump ring dangles on the chain to get the look you desire.

to string all the beaded beads and lampworked beads. End with the last beaded bead followed by a 6º.

[2] Cut two 5-in. (13 cm) pieces of chain.

[3] On each end of the beading wire, string a crimp bead, a wire guard, and an end link of a chain. String the wire back through the crimp bead, making sure each crimp bead is against the adjacent 6º. Crimp the crimp beads (Basics), and trim the tails. Using chainnose pliers, close a crimp cover over each crimp if desired.

Jump ring dangles

[1] Wrap the 22-gauge wire around the smallest step of the stepped roundnose pliers four or five times to make a coil **(photo a)**.

[2] Remove the coil from the pliers, and find the end of the wire at one end of the coil. This is the start of the first jump ring. Using flush cutters, cut the coil parallel to the end of the wire to separate the first jump ring **(photo b)**. Continue cutting one coil at a time until you have four or five small jump rings.

MATERIALS

necklace 18 in. (46 cm)
- **7** 12–14 mm lampworked beads
- **6 g** 3 mm drop beads
- **6 g** 6º seed beads
- **3 g** 11º cylinder beads
- **10 g** 15º seed beads
- **14** 3.5 x 5 mm bead aligners
- clasp
- 24 in. (61 cm) 22-gauge sterling silver wire, half-hard
- 10 in. (25 cm) chain, 6–7 mm links
- **2** crimp beads
- **2** crimp covers (optional)
- **2** wire guards
- Fireline 6 lb. test
- flexible beading wire, .019
- beading needles, #12
- **2** pairs of chainnose pliers
- crimping pliers
- stepped roundnose pliers
- flush wire cutters

[3] Repeat steps 1 and 2 until you have 20–30 small jump rings.

[4] To create medium jump rings, coil the wire around the medium step of the pliers as in step 1, and repeat steps 1 and 2 until you have 25–30 medium jump rings.

[5] Open a small jump ring (Basics), attach a drop bead and a link of a chain, and close the jump ring. Repeat to add a drop to every other link. Use the medium jump rings to attach 6°s to each link so that the rings hang opposite the small jump ring dangles.

[6] Open a medium jump ring, attach half of the clasp to an end link of a chain, and close the jump ring. Repeat on the other chain.

Jessica modified her design to display a larger focal bead, using only four beaded beads and two 12–14 mm lampworked beads.

Get to the point

Daisy chain unites daggers, fringe drops, and rose monteés for a necklace that's both feminine and edgy

designed by **Stephanie Eddy**

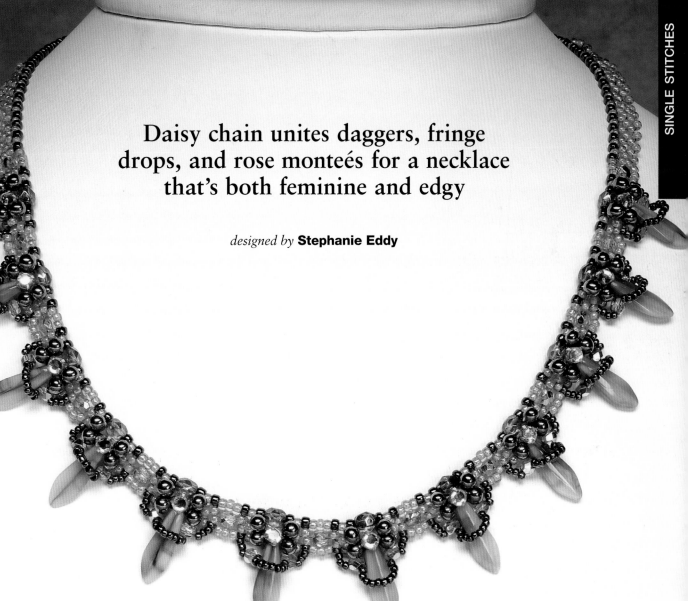

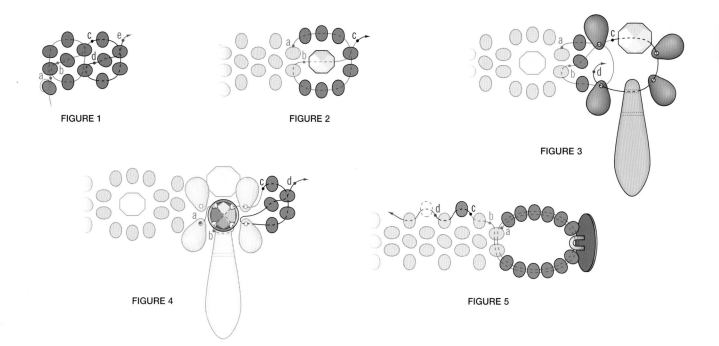

FIGURE 1

FIGURE 2

FIGURE 3

FIGURE 4

FIGURE 5

Take advantage of two-hole components for a richly layered necklace. Double-drilled daggers and cross-hole rose monteés allow you to add embellishments, change direction, and create a necklace that adds another dimension to classic daisy chain.

MATERIALS

necklace 18 in. (46 cm)

- **12** 15 mm two-hole daggers
- **12** 3–4 mm rose monteés
- **12** 4 mm fire-polished beads
- **37** 3 mm fire-polished beads
- **48** fringe drops
- **11º** seed beads
  10 g color A
  3 g color B
- **3 g** 15º seed beads
- shank button
- Fireline 6 lb. test
- beading needles, #12

stepbystep

[1] On a comfortable length of Fireline, attach a stop bead (Basics), leaving a 2-yd. (1.8 m) tail. Pick up six color A 11º seed beads, and sew through the first A again to form a ring (**figure 1, a–b**). Pick up an A, skip two As in the ring, and sew through the next A in the opposite direction (**b–c**).

[2] Pick up four As, and sew through the next A in the previous ring to form a six-bead ring (**c–d**). Pick up an A, skip two As in the ring, and sew through the next A in the opposite direction (**d–e**).

[3] Pick up eight As, and sew through the next A in the previous stitch (**figure 2, a–b**). Pick up a 3 mm fire-polished bead, skip four As in the ring, and sew through the fifth A in the opposite direction (**b–c**).

[4] Pick up an A, two fringe drops, and an A, and sew through the next A in the previous stitch (**figure 3, a–b**). Pick up an A, skip two As, and sew through the first drop in the opposite direction (**b–c**). Pick up a 4 mm fire-polished bead, two drops, and the top hole of a two-hole dagger, and sew through the next drop in the previous stitch (**c–d**). As you pull the stitches tight, make sure the drops are positioned on the front of the necklace.

[5] Pick up a rose monteé, slide it up to the beadwork, and sew through the top hole of the dagger to make a diagonal thread path (**figure 4, a–b**). Sew through the other hole in the rose monteé, and through the top drop on the other side of the ring (**b–c**).

[6] Pick up four As, and sew through the next drop in the previous stitch. Pick up an A, skip a drop and an A, and sew through the next A in the opposite direction (**c–d**). Make sure the drops are positioned on the front of the necklace.

[7] Repeat steps 3–6 until you've added a total of 12 daggers, ending and adding thread (Basics) as needed. Repeat step 3 to add another stitch with a 3 mm. Resume stitching in regular daisy chain, as in step 2, until the regular daisy chain segment is about 4 in. (10 cm) long.

[8] Remove the stop bead from the tail, and stitch in regular daisy chain until the segment is about 4 in. (10 cm) long.

[9] At one end of the necklace, pick up six As, the button shank, and six As. Sew through both As on the end of the last stitch, and retrace the thread path through the beads (**figure 5, a–b**). Sew through the top A on the last daisy chain stitch (**b–c**). Pick up a color B 11º seed bead, and sew through the next top A (**c–d**). Repeat until you reach the first daisy stitch with a 3 mm.

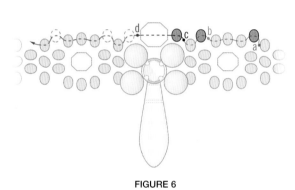

FIGURE 6

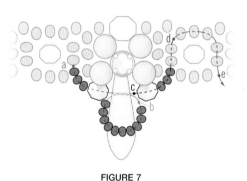

FIGURE 7

[10] Pick up a B, and sew through the three As on top of the next stitch (figure 6, a–b). Pick up a B, and sew through the next top A (b–c). Pick up a B, and sew through the 4 mm (c–d). Continue adding Bs, sewing through the top bead or beads of each stitch, until you reach the other end of the necklace.

[11] Pick up enough As to fit around the button, and sew through the two As at the end of the necklace to make a loop. Retrace the thread path.

[12] Sew through the beadwork to exit the two As between the first 3 mm stitch and the first stitch with drops (figure 7, point a). Pick up three 15º seed beads and a 3 mm, and sew through the bottom hole of the next dagger (a–b). Pick up 10 15ºs, and sew through the bottom hole of the dagger again, making a loop in front (b–c). Pick up a 3 mm and three 15ºs, and sew up through the two As between the next set of drops and the next 3 mm stitch (c–d). Sew through the next five As around the stitch (d–e).

[13] Repeat step 12 to embellish the remaining daggers. End the threads.

Flowers
and lace

Embellish a triangle stitch base to make a gently draping floral bib

designed by **Ludmila Raitzin**

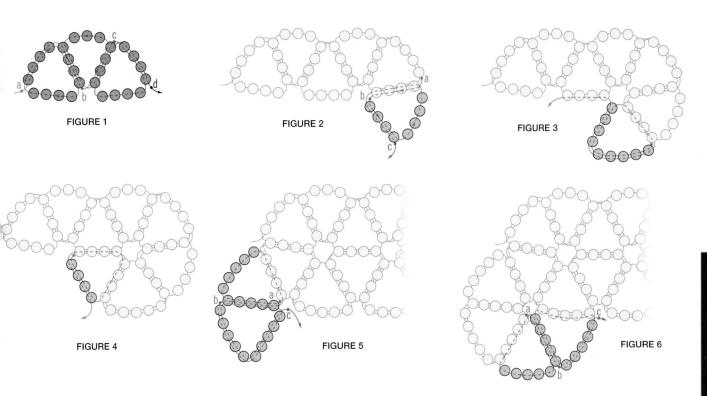

FIGURE 1

FIGURE 2

FIGURE 3

FIGURE 4

FIGURE 5

FIGURE 6

An alternating arrangement of triangles creates six-sided flower shapes that are perfect for embellishing with fire-polished beads.

stepbystep

Necklace base

Row 1

[1] On a comfortable length of Fireline, pick up 12 11º seed beads, and sew through the first eight 11ºs again (figure 1, a–b).

[2] Pick up seven 11ºs, and sew through the last four 11ºs your thread exited in the previous step and the first four 11ºs just added (b–c). This creates a triangle with three 11ºs along the top edge.

[3] Pick up eight 11ºs, and sew through the last four 11ºs your thread exited in the previous step and the first four 11ºs just added (c–d). This creates a triangle with four 11ºs along the bottom edge.

[4] Repeat steps 2 and 3 until the strip is about 16 in. (41 cm) or the desired necklace length, ending and adding thread (Basics) as needed. The strip will curve due to the difference in the number of beads along the top and bottom edges.

Row 2

[1] Sew through the bottom four 11ºs of the last triangle in row 1 (figure 2, a–b).

[2] Pick up eight 11ºs, sew through the four 11ºs in the previous row again, and continue through the first four 11ºs just added (b–c).

[3] Pick up nine 11ºs, and sew through the four 11ºs your thread exited in the previous stitch, the nine 11ºs just added, and the next four 11ºs in the previous row (figure 3).

[4] Pick up four 11ºs, and sew through the last four 11ºs added in the previous stitch, the last four 11ºs your thread exited in the previous row, and the four new 11ºs (figure 4).

[5] Repeat steps 3 and 4 along the length of row 1.

Row 3

[1] Pick up 10 11ºs, and sew through the last four 11ºs your thread exited in the previous row and the first five 11ºs just added (figure 5, a–b).

MATERIALS

necklace 17 in. (43 cm)

• 5 mm rondelle (to fill center flower – optional)
• 80–90 4 mm fire-polished beads in each of 3 colors: A, B, C
• 55 3 mm fire-polished beads, color D
• 25 g 11º seed beads
• Fireline 6 lb. test
• beading needles, #12

[2] Pick up 10 11ºs, and sew through the five 11ºs your thread exited in the previous stitch, and the 10 new 11ºs (b–c).

[3] Pick up 10 11ºs, and sew through the last five 11ºs your thread exited in the previous stitch and the first five 11ºs just added (figure 6, a–b).

[4] Pick up five 11ºs, and sew through the next five 11ºs in the previous row, the five side 11ºs in the previous stitch, and the five 11ºs just added (b–c).

[5] Repeat steps 3 and 4 along the length of row 2. At the very end of the row, you'll need to add one extra triangle to match the starting end. End the thread.

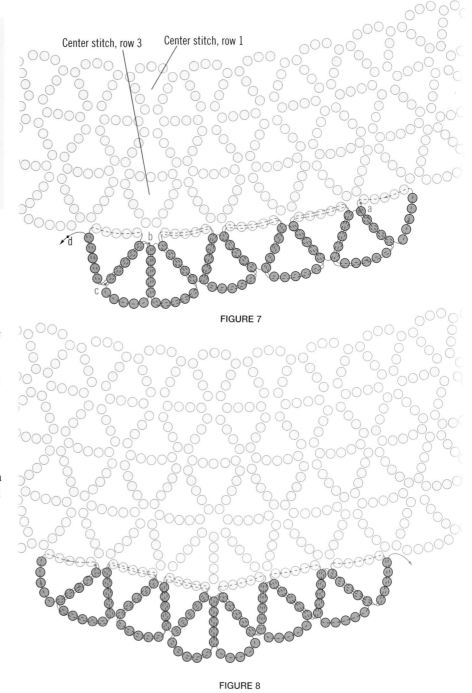

Center stitch, row 3   Center stitch, row 1

FIGURE 7

FIGURE 8

Row 4

[1] Identify the center stitch in row 1. If the center stitch does not have three beads along the top edge, choose one of the adjacent stitches. This will be the center point of the necklace. Find the stitch in row 3 that is directly below the one you just identified as the center in row 1. Count seven stitches to one side. Add a new thread in the beadwork, and exit the seventh stitch from the center, with the needle pointing toward the center of the necklace.

[2] Work eight stitches as in row 3 **(figure 7, a–b)**. Work one additional stitch with 10 11°s **(b–c)** to add an extra triangle in the central flower, then finish the flower motif with a stitch using five 11°s **(c–d)**.

[3] Work six more stitches as in row 3 to complete the row.

Row 5

[1] Sew through the beadwork to exit the fourth stitch from the end of row 4, with the needle pointing toward the center of the necklace.

[2] Work 12 stitches as in row 4 **(figure 8)**.

Embellishment

[1] Begin adding the fire-polished beads in the middle of the top row: Sew through the beadwork to exit a middle 11° of a triangle along the outer edge of the flower shape. Pick up a color A 4 mm fire-polished bead, cross the empty space in the middle of the stitch, and sew through an adjacent "wall" of 11°s and the next two 11°s in the outer edge **(figure 9)**. Repeat around to fill each triangle of the flower shape with a 4 mm.

[2] To fill the center of the flower, sew through the beadwork to exit a bead in the center circle, pick up a 3 mm fire-polished bead, and sew through the opposite "wall" of 11°s **(figure 10)**.

[3] Repeat steps 1 and 2 to add flowers along the length of the necklace. Alternate them in a zigzagging fashion, using colors A, B, and C as desired. When you fill the center flower, you'll need to add seven 4 mms. If desired,

use a 5 mm rondelle in the middle of the center flower. Fill in the area below the center flower as desired. End all remaining threads.

Clasp
Flower bead

[1] On 2 ft. (61 cm) of Fireline, pick up five 11°s, leaving a 6-in. (15 cm) tail. Tie the beads into a ring with a square knot (Basics).

[2] Pick up one 3 mm and four 11ºs. Skip the four 11ºs, sew back through the 3 mm, and continue through the next 11º in the ring (figure 11, a–b). Repeat around four times (b–c), and sew through the first 3 mm and four 11ºs again (c–d).

[3] Pick up a 3 mm, and sew through the next four 11ºs (figure 12, a–b). Repeat around, but in the last stitch, sew through only two 11ºs (b–c).

[4] Pick up a 3 mm and an 11º, skip the 11º, and sew back through the 3 mm. Sew through the next pair of 11ºs, the next 3 mm, and the following pair of 11ºs (figure 13, a–b). Repeat four times (b–c), then step up through the first 3 mm and 11º (c–d). Sew through the five 11ºs added in the round several times to pull the beads into a button shape, and end the thread.

[5] Add a new 18-in. (46 cm) thread at one end of the necklace base. Pick up eight 11ºs, sew through the center of the flower bead, and pick up one 11º. Skip the last 11º, and sew back through the flower bead, the eight 11ºs, and the bead your thread exited in the base. Retrace the thread path several times, and end the thread.

Loop

Add 18 in. (46 cm) of thread at the other end of the necklace, and pick up enough 11ºs to fit around the flower bead. Sew through two beads in the base to form a ring. Work a round of peyote stitch (Basics), retrace the thread path through the loop at least once, and end the thread.

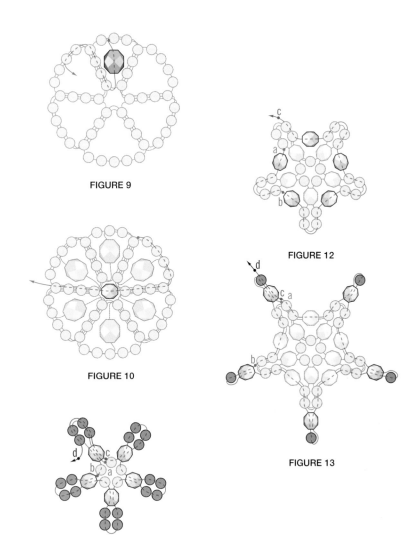

FIGURE 9

FIGURE 12

FIGURE 10

FIGURE 13

FIGURE 11

Make a cute flower-shaped beaded bead to finish off your necklace.

Fuse box

Hang a fused-glass pendant from a chain of seed beads in coordinating colors

designed by **Anna Elizabeth Draeger**

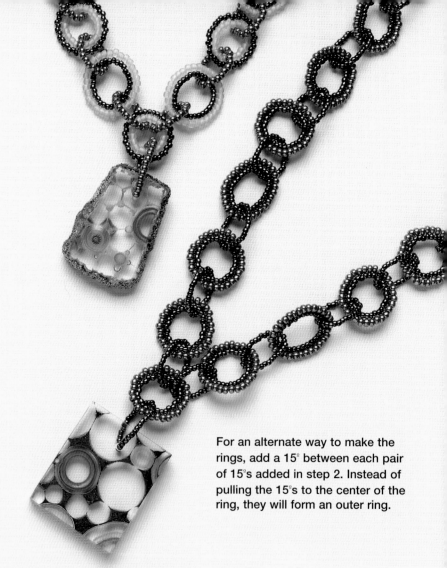

For an alternate way to make the rings, add a 15° between each pair of 15°s added in step 2. Instead of pulling the 15°s to the center of the ring, they will form an outer ring.

MATERIALS

necklace 17 in. (43 cm)

- 1¼ x 1¹⁄₁₆-in. (3.2 x 2.7 cm) fused-glass pendant (James Daschbach, lilyrosebeads.com)
- 5–8 g 11º seed beads
- 4–7 g 15º seed beads
- clasp
- Fireline 6 lb. test, or nylon beading thread, size D
- beading needles, #12

stepbystep

[1] On 1 yd. (.9 m) of Fireline or thread, pick up 30 11º seed beads, leaving a 4-in. (10 cm) tail. Sew through all the beads again, and continue through the first 11º. Gently pull the beads into a ring.

[2] Pick up a 15º seed bead, and sew through the 11º your thread exited at the start of this step and the next 11º in the ring (photo a). Repeat until you've added a 15º to each 11º in the ring.

[3] Sew through the first five 15ºs added. Pull gently to bring the 15ºs to the center of the ring of 11ºs (photo b). Sew through the next few 15ºs, and pull. Continue in this manner, and retrace the thread path through the 15ºs.

[4] Sew through the ring of 11ºs to exit next to the tail, and tie the threads together with a square knot (Basics). Sew through the next few 11ºs, and pull the knot into the adjacent 11º. Trim the working thread and tail.

[5] Repeat steps 1–4 to make the desired number of links.

[6] To connect the links, pick up 30 15ºs on 12 in. (30 cm) of thread. Sew through two links, and tie a square knot to form the beads into a ring (photo c). Retrace the thread path several times, and end the threads (Basics).

[7] Connect the pendant to the center link and the clasp halves to each end link as in step 6, but adjust the number of 15ºs picked up to accommodate the pendant and clasp.

a

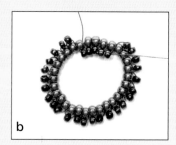

b

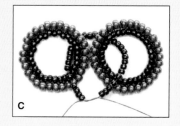

c

Autumn
garland

**Vintage-style flowers
herald the gorgeous
colors of fall**

designed by **Maria Kirk**

necklace 20 in. (51 cm)

- **7** 30–40 mm Lucite leaves
- **7** 26–30 mm Lucite flowers
- **35–40** 14–30 mm Lucite leaves
- **25–30** 7–26 mm Lucite flowers
- 11–13 g 6º seed beads, color A
- 1–2 g 8º seed beads, color B
- 2–3 g 11º seed beads, color B
- 2–3 g 11º seed beads, color C
- 2–3 g 11º seed beads, color D
- lobster claw clasp
- **4** 5–6 mm jump rings
- nylon beading thread
- beading needles, #12 or #13
- **2** Bead Stoppers
- **2** pairs of pliers

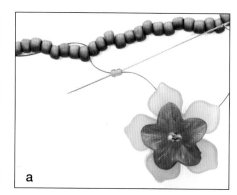

a

b

Having worked as a florist for many years, I find that most of my designs reflect my love of flowers and foliage. These Lucite flowers bunch beautifully around your neck, and their featherlight drape won't weigh you down.

stepbystep

[1] On 32 in. (81 cm) of thread, attach a Bead Stopper, leaving a 6-in. (15 cm) tail. String 6º seed beads for the desired necklace length, and attach a Bead Stopper, leaving at least 6 in. (15 cm) for the second tail.

[2] Tie a 1-yd. (.9 m) length of thread to the center of the beaded strand with an overhand knot (Basics).

[3] Using one end of the thread, pick up one to three 8º or 11º seed beads, a 26–30 mm flower, a 7–26 mm flower, and one to three seed beads. Sew back through the flowers and the first seed beads picked up **(photo a)**, then sew through the next 14 6ºs on the strand.

[4] Working as in step 3, attach three more flowers to one side of the central flower, varying the size, number, and color of seed beads picked up. Using the other end of the thread, attach three more flowers to the other side. With each end of the thread, sew through the remaining 6ºs on the strand, and secure the tails with the Bead Stoppers.

[5] Repeat step 2.

[6] With one end of the thread, exit a 6º a few beads away from the central flower. Pick up three to five seed beads, a 30–40 mm leaf, and two to four seed beads. Sew back through at least one of the first seed beads picked up **(photo b)**, then sew through the 6ºs to exit one or two beads from the next flower.

[7] Working as in step 6, and using both ends of the thread, attach a leaf for each flower, varying the size, number, and color of seed beads picked up. With

c

each end of the thread, sew through the remaining 6ºs on the strand, and secure the tails with the Bead Stoppers.

[8] Repeat step 2, and randomly attach the smaller flowers along the strand. Repeat to attach the smaller leaves. End these threads (Basics).

[9] Test the necklace for fit, and add or remove 6ºs if necessary. On one end, remove the Bead Stopper. With one tail, pick up 12–15 11º seed beads, sew back into the beaded strand, and end the thread. Repeat with the remaining tails, sewing through the same loop of beads.

EDITOR'S NOTE:
If you don't have Bead Stoppers, you can attach a stop bead (Basics) for each thread in the beaded strand.

Repeat on the other end of the necklace.

[10] On one end, open a jump ring (Basics), and attach the beaded loop. Close the jump ring. Attach a second jump ring and a lobster claw clasp **(photo c)**. On the other end of the necklace, attach two jump rings.

DESIGN NOTES:
• Before attaching the smaller flowers and leaves, divide them into two groups of roughly the same number and size. Then divide the groups in half again. Attach one group to half of the necklace at a time so that the overall look of the piece is balanced.

• You can mix up the colors of the flowers and leaves, or gradate the colors along the length of the necklace.

• If you find a floppy flower or leaf, try sewing through it again for added stability. Or add a smaller flower, leaf, or loop of seed beads behind it.

Crystal-caged pearls

Catch a glimpse of pearly luster within a woven coat of crystals and seed beads

designed by
Cathy Lampole

MATERIALS

necklace 20 in. (51 cm)

- **3** 14 mm pearls
- **8** 10 mm round crystals
- **2** 10 mm accent beads
- **40** 8 mm pearls
- **78** 4 mm bicone crystals
- **52** 4 mm fire-polished beads
- **60** 3 mm bicone crystals
- **3 g** 11º Japanese cylinder beads
- **2 g** 15º seed beads
- **2** 3 mm spacers
- clasp
- **2** crimp beads
- **2** crimp covers
- nylon beading thread or Fireline 6 lb. test
- flexible beading wire, .015
- beading needles, #12
- chainnose pliers
- crimping pliers
- wire cutters

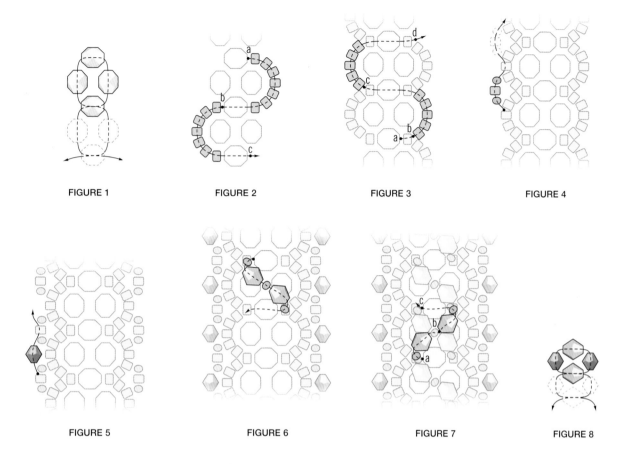

FIGURE 1   FIGURE 2   FIGURE 3   FIGURE 4

FIGURE 5   FIGURE 6   FIGURE 7   FIGURE 8

stepbystep

Large bead

[1] Thread a needle on each end of 1½ yd. (1.4 m) of thread, and center a 4 mm fire-polished bead. With each needle, pick up a fire-polished. With one needle, pick up a fire-polished, and cross the other needle through it (**figure 1**).

[2] Continue in crossweave technique until you have seven beads along each edge of the strip and eight in the center. With each needle, pick up a fire-polished, and cross the needles through the first fire-polished to form a ring.

[3] With one needle, pick up seven cylinder beads, and sew through the next parallel fire-polished, skipping the edge fire-polished and forming an arc around it (**figure 2, a–b**). Repeat (**b–c**) around the ring,

so that the arcs alternate on each side of the ring. Sew through the first cylinder added in this step (**figure 3, a–b**), pick up five cylinders, and, working in the opposite direction, sew through the last cylinder in the next group on the same side of the ring, the next fire-polished, and the next cylinder (**b–c**). Repeat (**c–d**) around the ring, and exit the center cylinder of an arc.

[4] Pick up a 15º seed bead, a cylinder, and a 15º, and sew through the center cylinder of the next arc (**figure 4**). Repeat around the ring, and exit the first cylinder added in this step. With the other needle, sew through the beadwork to exit the center cylinder of an arc on the other side of the ring, and repeat.

[5] Working one side of the ring at a time, pick up a

3 mm bicone crystal, and sew through the next cylinder added in the previous round (**figure 5**). Repeat around the ring, and pull the beads snug. Sew through all the beads in the last round again. Insert the 14 mm pearl so the hole is centered in the opening, and repeat on the other side of the ring with the other needle, enclosing the pearl.

[6] With one needle, sew through the beadwork to exit a center fire-polished. Pick up a 15º, a 4 mm bicone crystal, a 15º, a 4 mm bicone, and a 15º. Cross over the center round at a diagonal, and sew through the next parallel fire-polished (**figure 6**). Repeat around the ring, and end the thread (Basics).

[7] Using the remaining thread, sew through the beadwork to exit a center fire-polished. Pick up a 15º

and a 4 mm bicone, and sew through the center 15º of the adjacent stitch (**figure 7, a–b**). Pick up a 4 mm and a 15º, and sew through the next parallel fire-polished (**b–c**). Repeat around the ring, and end the thread.

[8] Repeat steps 1–7 to make a second large bead.

Small bead

[1] Thread a needle on each end of 1½ yd. (1.4 m) of thread, and center a 4 mm bicone. With each needle, pick up a 3 mm bicone. With one needle, pick up a 4 mm bicone, and cross the other needle through it (**figure 8**). Continue in crossweave

43

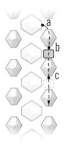

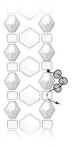
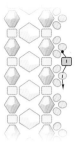
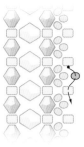
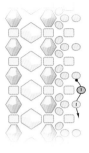

FIGURE 9   FIGURE 10   FIGURE 11   FIGURE 12   FIGURE 13

technique following the established pattern until you have 13 3 mms along each edge and 14 4 mm bicones in the center. With each needle, pick up a 3 mm, and cross the needles through the first 4 mm bicone to form a ring.

[2] Working with one needle at a time, sew through an edge 3 mm **(figure 9, a–b)**. Pick up a cylinder, and sew through the next 3 mm **(b–c)**. Repeat around the ring, and exit the first cylinder added. Repeat on the other side with the other needle.

[3] With one needle, pick up three 15°s, and sew through the next cylinder **(figure 10)**. Repeat around the ring, and step up to exit the center 15° of the first arc.

[4] Pick up a cylinder, and sew through the next center 15° **(figure 11)**. Repeat around the ring, pulling the beads snug, and exit the first cylinder added in this round.

[5] Pick up a 15°, and sew through the next cylinder **(figure 12)**. Repeat around the ring, and exit the first 15° added in this round.

[6] Pick up a 15°, and sew through the next 15° in the previous round **(figure 13)**. Repeat around the ring, and end the thread.

[7] Insert the 14 mm pearl so the hole is centered in the opening, and repeat steps 3–6 to finish the other side of the bead.

Necklace

[1] Cut a 26-in. (66 cm) piece of beading wire, and center eight 10 mm round crystals. On each end, string a 10 mm accent bead.

[2] On one end, string an 8 mm pearl, a large beaded bead, an 8 mm, the small beaded bead, an 8 mm, a large beaded bead, and 14 8 mms. On the other end, string 23 8 mms.

[3] On each end, string a crimp bead, two 4 mm bicones, a 3 mm spacer, and half of the clasp. Go back through the spacers, 4 mm bicones, and crimp beads. Test the fit, and add or remove beads as necessary. Crimp the crimp beads (Basics), and trim the wires. Close a crimp cover over each crimp with chainnose pliers.

Fanciful
romance

Turn up the heat with fire-polished beads, and fan the flames of fantasy

designed by **Jeka Lambert**

Evoke Victorian romanticism with the surprising simplicity of five connected fans. A sixth fan doubles as a special touch at the nape of the neck as well as a closure.

stepbystep

If you are using only one color of 5 x 7 mm fire-polished drop beads, use them for every mention of an A or a B.

Brick stitch fans

[1] On 1 yd. (.9 m) of thread, pick up an 8 mm round bead, leaving a 6-in. (15 cm) tail. Sew through the 8 mm two more times in the same direction, leaving two thread loops **(figure 1)**. Snug the thread loops next to each other and close to the bead, but don't pull them too tight.

[2] Pick up a color A 5 x 7 mm fire-polished drop bead, narrow end first, and another A, wide end first **(photo a)**. Sew under both thread loops **(photo b)**, positioning the As next to each other with the narrow ends facing the 8 mm. Sew through both As again **(figure 2, a–b)**, then sew under the thread loops, and through the second A **(b–c)**. Working in brick stitch (Basics), add a total of seven As to make the base of a fan.

[3] With your thread exiting the wide end of an end A, pick up two 8º seed beads, sew under the thread bridge between the first and second A, and sew through the second 8º again to begin brick stitch **(photo c)**. Continue in brick stitch, adding a third 8º to the first thread bridge, two 8ºs to the second, three 8ºs to the third, two 8ºs to the fourth, two 8ºs to the fifth, and three 8ºs to the sixth for a total of 15 8ºs. With your thread exiting an end 8º, sew through the next 8º, under the thread bridge, and back up through the second 8º to get into position for the next row.

[4] Pick up three 15º seed beads, and sew back through the 8º your thread just exited **(photo d)**. Snug up the beads to form a picot **(photo e)**. Sew through the next 8º.

[5] Repeat step 4 until you reach the eighth (middle) 8º.

[6] Pick up a 15º, a 4 x 6 mm rondelle, a 15º, a color B 5 x 7 mm fire-polished drop bead, narrow end first, and three 15ºs. Skip the last three 15ºs, and sew back through the beads just added **(photo f)**. Sew through the middle 8º and up through the next 8º.

[7] Repeat step 4 until you reach the 14th (second-to-last) 8º.

[8] Repeat steps 1–7 to make a total of six fans. End the working thread and tail (Basics) for five of the fans.

[9] For the sixth fan, exit an end 8º with the working thread. Pick up an 8º and enough 11º seed beads to form a loop that fits snugly around a 6 mm round bead, and sew back through the 8º just added **(photo g)**. Sew through the beadwork to exit the remaining edge 8º, and repeat for a second loop. Sew back and forth through the beadwork and both loops until it becomes difficult to sew through the beads. End the working thread and tail.

MATERIALS

necklace 18 in. (46 cm)

- **6** 8 mm round glass beads
- **8** 6 mm round glass beads
- 5 x 7 mm faceted fire-polished drop beads, drilled lengthwise
  42 color A
  6 color B
  (or **48** in a single color)
- **18** 4 x 6 mm rondelles
- 5 g 8º seed beads*
- 7 g 11º seed beads*
- 2 g 15º seed beads*
- nylon beading thread, size A, in a color to coordinate with the beads
- beading needles, #12

* all the same color

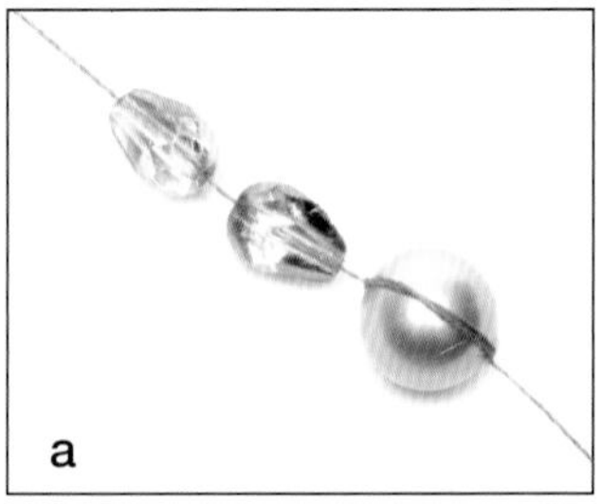

a

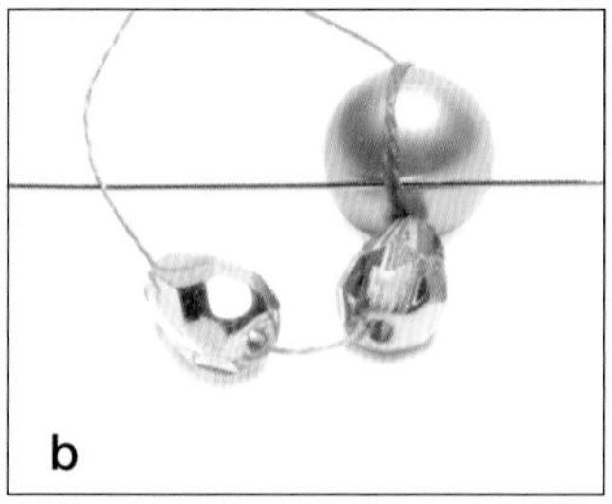

b

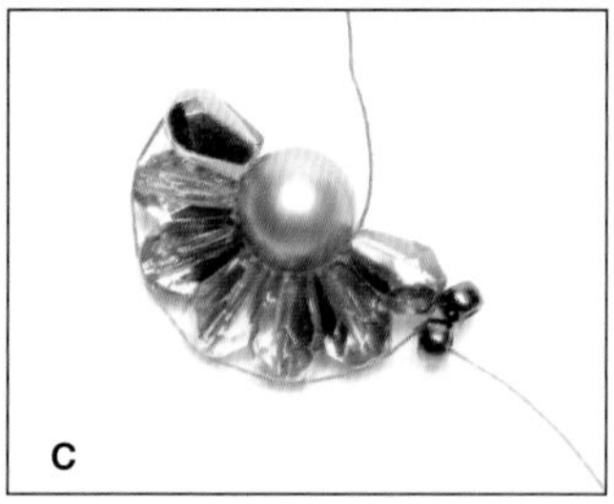

c

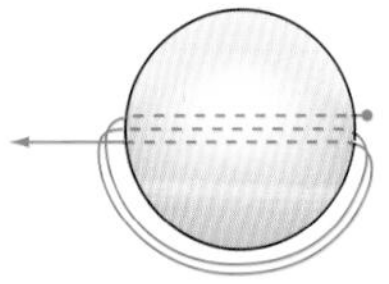

FIGURE 1

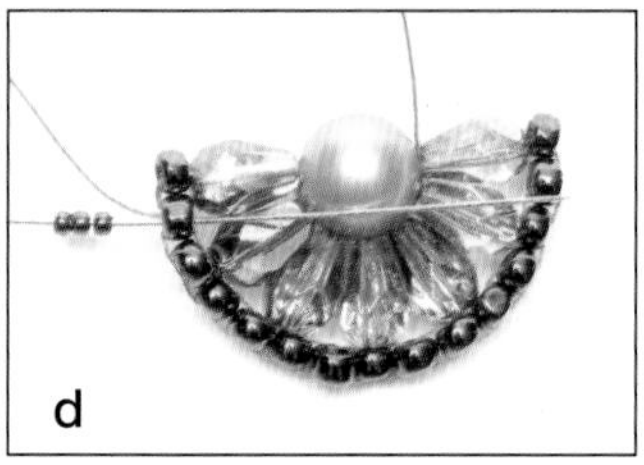

d

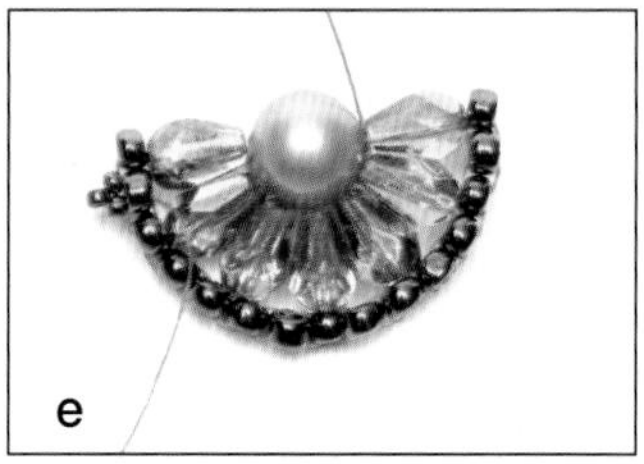

e

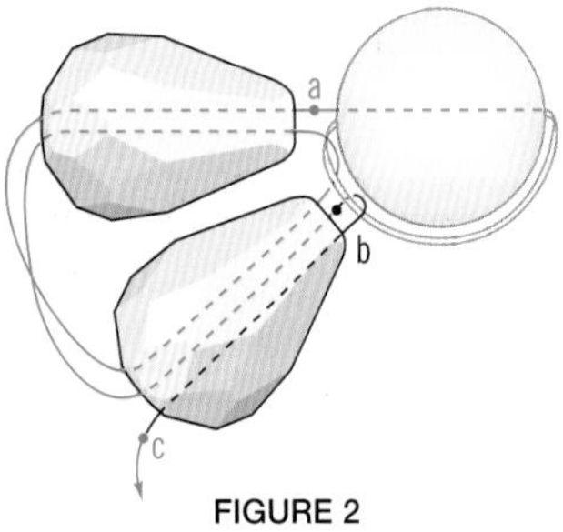

FIGURE 2

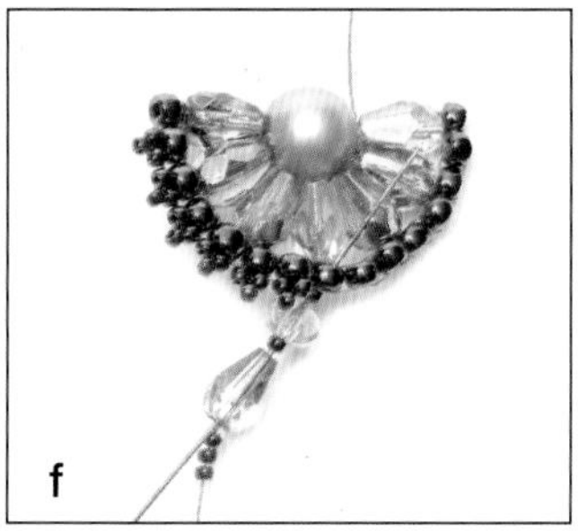

f

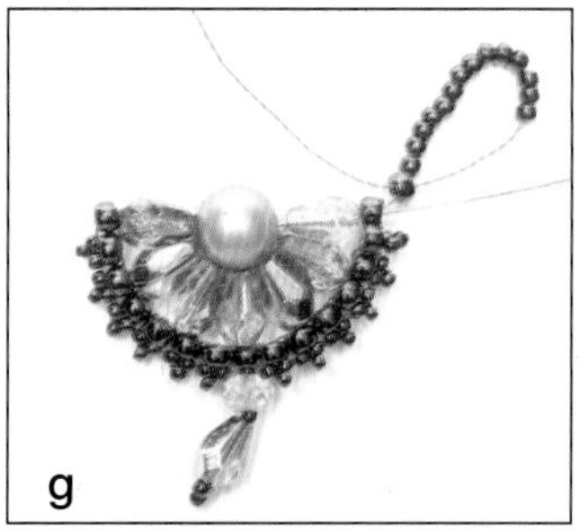

g

h

i

Peyote stitch ropes

[1] On 4 yd. (3.7 m) of thread, pick up seven 11°s, leaving a 1-yd. (.9 m) tail. Tie the beads into a ring with a square knot (Basics), leaving some slack, and sew through the first bead after the knot. Pick up an 11°, skip an 11° in the previous round, and sew through the next 11°. Working in tubular peyote stitch (Basics), make a rope that is 3¼ in. (8.3 cm) long, ending and adding thread (Basics) if needed.

[2] Sew through the beadwork to exit an up-bead at the end of the rope.

[3] Pick up an 11°, a 6 mm round bead, and an 11°. Skip the last 11° added, and sew back through the previous two beads added. Sew through the next up-bead at the end of the peyote stitch rope (photo h).

[4] Sew through the 11°, 6 mm, and 11° from step 3. Skip the last 11°, and sew back through the previous two beads. Sew through the next up-bead, and repeat. Sew through a few rows of the beadwork, and end the thread.

[5] Repeat steps 1–4 to make a second peyote stitch rope.

Assembly

[1] Thread a needle on the remaining tail at the end of a peyote stitch rope. Sew through the beadwork to exit an up-bead.

[2] Pick up an 8°, a rondelle, an 8°, a 6 mm, an 8°, a rondelle, and an 8°, and sew through a fan from one side to the other through the first 8°, A, 8 mm, A, and last 8° (photo i). Repeat the sequence until you have strung five fans. Pick up an 8°, a rondelle, an 8°, a 6 mm, an 8°, a rondelle, and an 8°.

[3] Sew through an up-bead at the end of the remaining peyote stitch rope. Sew back through the strung beads and fans, and sew through the next up-bead at the end of the first peyote stitch rope. Continue sewing through the up-beads and strung beads until you have sewn through two up-beads at the end of each peyote stitch rope. End the thread, and use the tail on the remaining peyote stitch rope to sew through the remaining up-beads. End the thread.

Grand
circles

MATERIALS

necklace 30 in. (76 cm)

- 8 10–12 mm coin pearls
- 9 4–5 mm pearls
- 17 g 8º hex-cut beads, color A
- 14 g 8º seed beads, color B
- 11º seed beads
  50 g color C
  5 g color D
- 2 g 11º cylinder beads, color E
- 15º seed beads
  2 g color F
  1 g color G
- Fireline 6 lb. test
- beading needles, #12

Concentric rings expand in proportion to beads of different sizes and shapes

designed by **Jonna Ellis Holston**

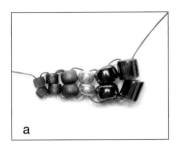

a

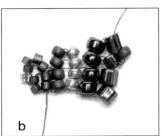

b

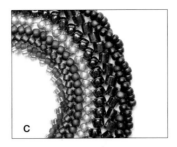

c

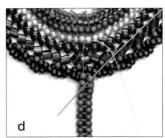

d

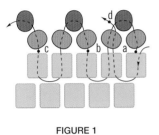

FIGURE 1

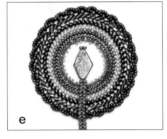

FIGURE 3

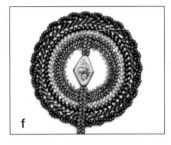

e

f

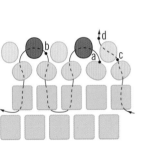

FIGURE 2

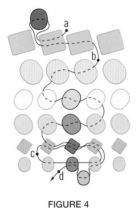

FIGURE 4

g

h

Ever-expanding rings are seen wherever you look — tree rings, ripples on the surface of a pond, or the bands around the planet Saturn. Stitch a beaded version of this phenomenon to add a little nature to your wardrobe.

stepbystep

Toggle bar

[1] On 2 yd. (1.8 m) of Fireline, attach a stop bead (Basics), leaving a 6-in. (15 cm) tail. Pick up 22 color A 8º hex-cut beads.
[2] Work eight rows of peyote stitch (Basics) for a total of 10 rows, and zip up (Basics) the edges to form a tube.

[3] With your thread exiting an end A 8º, pick up a D 11º seed bead, a C 11º seed bead, and a D, and sew down through an adjacent A and up through the next A (figure 1, a–b). Repeat once to form two picots (b–c).
[4] Pick up a D and a C, and sew down through the adjacent D and A and up through the next A and D (c–d).
[5] Pick up a C, and sew down through the next D and A and up through the

adjacent A and D (figure 2, a–b). Repeat once (b–c). Step up through a C (c–d).
[6] Pick up a D, and sew through an opposite C (figure 3, a–b). Sew through the five Cs to secure the ring (b–c).
[7] Sew through the beadwork to the other end, and repeat steps 3–6. End the thread (Basics).

Medallions

[1] On 3 yd. (2.7 m) of Fireline, pick up two color F 15º seed beads and two color E 11º cylinder beads, leaving a 24-in. (61 cm) tail. Sew through the four beads again, and snug them up to form two columns of two beads each.

[2] Working in ladder stitch (Basics), pick up two beads in each stitch: two Ds, two Cs, two color B 8º seed beads, and two As (photo a). Do not reinforce the thread path. With the tail, sew through the adjacent Es.
[3] Work three stitches in herringbone stitch (Basics), following the bead order of the first two rows.
[4] To make the turn (Basics), pick up a color G 15º seed bead, and sew up through the last F added.
[5] Repeat step 3.
[6] To make the turn, pick up a D, and sew up through the end A (photo b).

[7] Repeat steps 3–6 to work a total of 56 rows.

[8] To join the ends to form a ring, sew through the A on the starting end, pick up a D, and sew back through the A your thread exited at the start of this step and the previous A (figure 4, a–b). Snug up the beads.

[9] Sew across the edges, adding a bead appropriate to the row if needed to make the medallion lie flat (b–c). Retrace the thread path between the last two rounds, and add a G to the inner edge of the medallion (c–d). Sew through the beadwork, and exit an outer edge 11º.

[10] Pick up eight Cs or Ds, skip an edge 11º, and sew through the next edge 11º. Repeat around the medallion.

[11] Sew through the Bs to the next edge 11º without a loop. Pick up eight Cs or Ds, and sew from back to front through the next edge 11º without a loop. Repeat around the medallion (photo c). End the threads.

[12] Repeat steps 1–11 to make eight more medallions.

Connecting chains

[1] On 2 yd. (1.8 m) of Fireline, pick up four Cs, leaving a 24-in. (61 cm) tail. Sew through the beads again to form two columns of two beads each. Sew through the first two beads again.

[2] Working in modified herringbone stitch, pick up two Cs, and sew down through one C and up through two Cs. Repeat to make a chain 12 Cs long.

[3] Position a medallion on your work surface so that the seam is centered at the lower half of the circle.

[4] With the thread exiting the left C of the herringbone chain, sew through the D in the seam, and sew down through the C on the right edge of the chain (photo d). Snug the chain to the medallion, and sew up through the left C your thread exited at the start of this step.

[5] Work five to eight more stitches to center the coin pearl within the herringbone medallion. Pick up a coin pearl and two Cs, and sew back through the coin pearl and two or three Cs in the right edge of the chain. Sew up through two or three Cs on the left edge of the chain, the coin pearl, and the C on the left of the pair picked up in this step (photo e).

[6] Work the same number of stitches as the segment in step 5. Sew through the D across from the seam. Snug the chain to the medallion (photo f), and sew down through the C on the right edge of the chain, and sew up through the left C.

[7] Work 12 more stitches using Cs. Work one stitch using Ds.

[8] Pick up a 4–5 mm pearl and two Ds. Sew back through the 4–5 mm pearl and D, one or two Cs on the right edge of the chain (photo g), and up through the Cs and D on the left edge of the chain, the pearl, and the D on the left of the pair picked up in this step.

[9] Repeat steps 2–8 seven times to connect seven of the remaining eight medallions. End and add thread (Basics) as needed.

[10] To work the chain on the reverse side of the medallion, repeat steps 1–7 but sew through the pearls previously stitched into the front chain and the D flanking the 4–5 mm pearls (photo h).

[11] To connect the eighth medallion, repeat steps 2–4. Work seven stitches using Cs and one stitch using Ds. Pick up a C, and sew back through the adjacent D (photo i). Do not end the thread.

[12] Repeat step 11 on the reverse side of the eighth medallion, but sew through the end pair of Ds to close the loop. End the threads.

[13] On the other end, use the tail to work a stitch using Ds. Pick up a 4–5 mm pearl and two Ds. Sew back through the 4–5 mm pearl, down through the D on the right edge of the chain, and up through the D on the left edge of the chain, the pearl, and the D on the left of the pair picked up in this step.

[14] Work 18 stitches using Cs and one stitch using Ds. Sew through the center point of the toggle bar. Pick up a B, a D, a C, and a D, and sew back through the B, the center point of the toggle bar, and the D on the right edge of the chain. Retrace the thread path a few times, and end the thread (photo j).

[15] Attach the remaining chain on the reverse side of the end medallion to the toggle chain, sewing through the Ds and 4–5 mm pearl. Retrace the thread path, and end the thread.

Triple time

Create three identical
beaded ring components
to make a necklace that
combines stitching with
a bit of wirework

designed by **Cindy Pankopf**

Stitched rings act as links in a chain for a textured necklace that lets you use needles and pliers. Repeating different styles of links in a decorative chain creates a pattern that pulls it all together.

stepbystep

Beaded rings

[1] On 2 yd. (1.8 m) of conditioned thread or Fireline, center 24 11º seed beads, and tie them into a ring with a square knot (Basics). Sew through the first two beads again **(figure 1, a–b)**.

[2] Pick up two 11ºs, and sew through the two 11ºs your thread exited and the two new 11ºs again **(b–c)**. Pick up two 11ºs, and sew through the next two 11ºs in the previous round and the two new 11ºs **(c–d)**. Continue around, working in square stitch (Basics), and end by sewing through the first two 11ºs added in this round **(d–e)**.

[3] Pick up two 11ºs, and sew through the two 11ºs your thread exited and the two new 11ºs again **(figure 2, a–b)**. Pick up a fringe drop and two 11ºs, and sew through the next two 11ºs in the previous round and the two 11ºs just picked up **(b–c)**. Continue around in modified square stitch, picking up a drop and two 11ºs for each stitch **(c–d)**. Pick up a drop, and sew through the first two 11ºs added in this round **(d–e)**.

[4] Repeat step 3 with the tail, stitching a round of drops and 11ºs off the first round. The drops should align around the edges.

[5] With your thread exiting a pair of 11ºs, pick up a 15º seed bead, a drop, and a 15º, and sew through the two 11ºs your thread exited and the three beads just added **(figure 3, a–b)**. Pick up an 11º, and sew through the next drop bead in the previous round and the 11º just added **(b–c)**. Repeat around, and sew through the first three beads added in this round. End the thread (Basics).

[6] With the remaining thread exiting a pair of 11ºs on the other edge, sew through the corresponding 15º, drop, and 15º added in step 5. Sew through the five beads again, and continue through the next 11º added in the previous step. Sew through the adjacent drop and the 11º. Work around the ring using a square stitch thread path, sewing through the beads previously added **(figure 4)**. End the thread.

[7] Repeat steps 1–6 to make two more beaded rings.

Necklace assembly

[1] Open an 8 mm jump ring (Basics), and slide it between the two inner and three outer rounds of a beaded ring. Attach a large decorative chain link, and close the jump ring. Repeat twice, for a total of three links spaced equally around the ring **(photo a)**.

MATERIALS

necklace 24 in. (61 cm)
- 10–15 3–8 mm accent beads or spacers
- 5 g 3 mm fringe drops
- 5 g 11º seed beads
- 2 g 15º Japanese seed beads
- lobster claw clasp
- 10 in. (25 cm) 24-gauge wire
- 20 in. (51 cm) decorative chain, plus 3 additional decorative chain links
- 7 8 mm outside diameter (OD) jump rings
- 3 5 mm OD jump rings
- 5 3 mm OD jump rings
- Fireline 8 lb. test
- beading needles, #12
- chainnose pliers
- roundnose pliers
- wire cutters

a

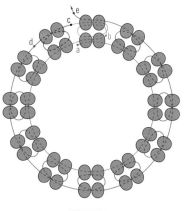

FIGURE 1

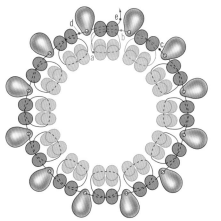

FIGURE 2

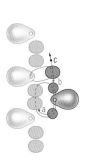

FIGURE 3

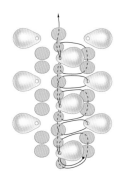

FIGURE 4

b

d

c

[2] Open an 8 mm jump ring, attach the other end of a decorative link from step 1 and a beaded ring, and close the jump ring. Repeat with the remaining beaded ring.

[3] Cut a 9-in. (23 cm) piece of decorative chain. Open an 8 mm jump ring, slide it through one of the beaded rings, directly across from the decorative link, and attach the end link of the chain. Close the jump ring.

[4] Repeat step 3, attaching the chain to the other beaded ring **(photo b)**.

[5] Open a 5 mm jump ring, attach the lobster claw clasp and the end link of the chain from step 3, and close the jump ring. Open a 5 mm jump ring, attach the end link of the other chain, and close the jump ring.

[6] Cut a 2-in. (5 cm) piece of 24-gauge wire, and make the first half of a wrapped loop (Basics). Slide a drop into the loop, and complete the wraps. String two to five accent beads and spacers, and make the first half of a wrapped loop. Slide a 3 mm jump ring into the loop, and complete the wraps **(photo c)**. Repeat to make a total of five dangles.

[7] Cut a 1-in. (2.5 cm) piece of chain. Open the jump rings of four of the dangles, and attach them along the length of the chain, starting with an end link. Close the jump rings. Open a 5 mm jump ring, attach the remaining dangle, the other end link of the chain, and the decorative link at the bottom of the necklace. Close the jump ring **(photo d)**.

Elementary engineering

Multiple components work in concert to showcase an art-glass bead focal

designed by **Jimmie Boatright**

Structure natural and organic-looking elements with beads in a variety of shapes and sizes for a necklace with chemistry.

stepbystep

Peyote rings
Side one

[1] On 1 yd. (.9 m) of Fireline, center 48 15º seed beads. Tie the beads into a ring with a square knot (Basics), and sew through the first bead again. These beads will shift to form the first two rounds in the next step.

[2] With one end of the thread, work two rounds of tubular peyote stitch (Basics) using 15ºs, stepping up at the end of each round.

[3] Work a round of peyote stitch with 11º cylinder beads, stepping up at the end of the round.

[4] Work a round of peyote stitch as follows: Work two stitches with cylinders, then work a stitch with an 11º seed bead. Repeat these three stitches to complete the round, and step up.

[5] Work a round of peyote stitch as follows: Work one stitch with a cylinder and two stitches with 11ºs. Repeat these three stitches to complete the round, and step up.

[6] Work a round of peyote stitch as follows: Work one stitch with an 11º, one stitch with a color A 8º seed bead, and one stitch with an 11º. Repeat these three stitches to complete the round. Tie a couple of half-hitch knots (Basics), but do not trim the thread.

Side two

[1] With the other thread, exit a 15º in round 1, and work two rounds of peyote stitch with 15ºs, stepping up at the end of each round.

[2] Repeat steps 3–5 of "Side one," making sure to match the pattern.

[3] Zip up (Basics) the edges of the ring. End the threads (Basics).

[4] Make a second peyote ring.

Bezeled coins

[1] On 1 yd. (.9 m) of Fireline, sew through the center hole of a mosaic shell coin bead, leaving a 12-in. (30 cm) tail. Pick up an even number of cylinder beads to fit around half of the coin. For a 17 mm coin, I used 22 cylinders.

[2] Sew through the coin, and pick up the same

Incorporate a wide variety of shapes, sizes, and styles of beads for this stash-busting necklace.

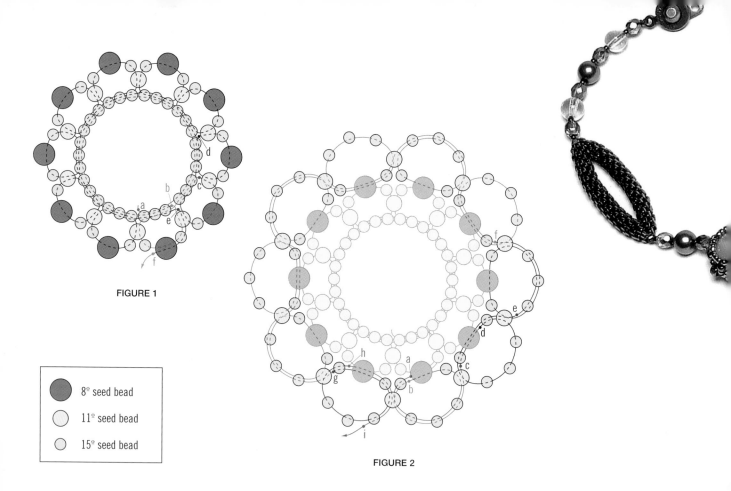

FIGURE 1

FIGURE 2

Key:

● 8º seed bead

○ 11º seed bead

○ 15º seed bead

number of cylinders picked up in step 1. Sew through the coin again.

[3] Sew through all the cylinders around the coin to form a ring.

[4] Work one round of peyote stitch with cylinders, then work two rounds of peyote stitch with 15ºs.

[5] Sew through the beadwork to exit a cylinder in the first round of cylinders. Work two rounds of peyote stitch with cylinders toward the other side of the coin, then work two rounds of peyote stitch with 15ºs.

[6] Sew through the beadwork to exit the center round along the edge of the coin, pick up an 11º, and sew through the next cylinder in the round. Repeat to complete the round. End the working thread and tail.

[7] Make a second bezeled coin.

Caged beads

[1] On 1 yd. (.9 m) of Fireline, pick up 30 15ºs, leaving a 6-in. (15 cm) tail. Sew through all the beads again to form a ring, and sew through the next three 15ºs **(figure 1, a–b)**.

[2] Pick up an 11º seed bead, a 15º, a color B 8º seed bead, a 15º, and an 11º, and sew through the 15º the tail

is exiting and the next five beads in the original ring **(b–c)**.

[3] Pick up an 11º, a 15º, a B, and a 15º, and sew through the adjacent 11º in the previous stitch and the next six 15ºs in the original ring **(c–d)**. Repeat this step to complete the round **(d–e)**.

[4] Sew through the first 11º, 15º, and 8º added in the first stitch of this round **(e–f)**.

[5] Pick up a 15º, an 11º, three 15ºs, an 11º, and a 15º, and sew through the B your thread exited at the start of this step **(figure 2, a–b)**. Continue through the first six beads just added **(b–c)**.

[6] Pick up a 15º, and sew through the next B **(c–d)**. Pick up a 15º, an 11º, and three 15ºs, and sew through the 11º in the previous stitch, and the next 15º, B, 15º, and 11º in this stitch **(d–e)**.

[7] Pick up three 15ºs, an 11º, and a 15º, and sew back through the next B. Pick up a 15º, and sew through the adjacent 11º in the previous stitch and the three 15ºs and 11º just added **(e–f)**.

[8] Repeat steps 6 and 7 three times **(f–g)**. For the last stitch, pick up a 15º, and sew through the next B. Pick up a 15º, and sew through the adjacent 11º in the first stitch. Pick up three 15ºs,

and sew through the 11º added in the previous stitch and the first 15º added in this stitch **(g–h)**. Sew through the next five beads to exit the outer edge **(h–i)**.

[9] Insert a 12 mm bead into the cage, and sew through all the 15ºs along the outer edge several times to snug up the cage, holding the 12 mm in place. Locate the hole in the 12 mm, and sew through it to secure the bead to the cage. End the working thread and tail.

[10] Make a second caged bead.

Assembly

The necklace is assembled using doubled thread to connect the components. The fringe is made using single thread.

[1] Add 1 yd. (.9 m) of doubled Fireline to a caged bead (Basics), exiting a B along the edge of the cage. Starting and ending with an 11º, pick up 1½ in. (3.8 cm) of 3–8 mm beads alternating with 11ºs. Pick up seven 15ºs and half of the clasp. Skip the 15ºs, and sew back through the beads just strung and an edge B in the bead cage. Sew through the beadwork to exit a B opposite the one your thread exited at the start of this step.

[2] Starting and ending with an 11º, pick up 1 in. (2.5 cm) of 3–8 mm beads

Incorporate stitched oval links instead of the 15 x 30 mm flat oval gemstones for a lighter weight alternative.

MATERIALS

amazonite necklace 21 in. (53 cm)

- art-glass bead (Joanne Morash, blueirisdesigns.com)
- **4** 15 x 30 mm flat oval gemstone beads (amazonite)
- **2** 15–18 mm mosaic shell coin beads
- **2** 12 mm round beads (green agate)
- **80–90** 3–8 mm assorted beads: round glass beads, fire-polished beads, gemstone beads, coin beads
- 1 g 8º seed beads in each of **2** colors: A (Miyuki 8-389A, fuchsia-lined cranberry AB), B (Miyuki 8-2035, matte metallic khaki iris)
- 4–6 g 11º seed beads (Miyuki 0577, dyed butter cream silver-lined alabaster)
- 6–8 g 11º cylinder beads (DB0380, matte metallic khaki iris)
- 6–8 g 15º seed beads (Toho 15R71, nickel-plated silver)
- S-hook clasp with **2** 6 mm soldered jump rings
- Fireline 6 lb. test
- beading needles, #12

bronze necklace colors:

- 20 mm and 12 mm art-glass bead (Rodney Andrew, randrewglass.com)
- 3–8 mm assorted beads in neutral and metallic tones
- 8º seed beads (Miyuki 342, berry-lined light topaz AB)
- 11º seed beads (Miyuki 2006, bronze)
- 11º cylinder beads
  color A used in rings (DB802, dyed shell silk satin)
  color B used in bezeled coins and pointed oval links (DB26, metallic steel iris)
- 15º seed beads (Toho 15R7119, nickel-plated silver)

alternating with cylinders. Sew through an edge 11º in a bezeled coin and back through the beads just strung. Pick up an 11º, and sew through the B in the bead cage. Retrace the thread path through the connection a few times, and end the thread.

[3] Add 12–18 in. (30–40 cm) of doubled Fireline to the bezeled coin, exiting an 11º opposite the previous connection. Starting and ending with a 15º, pick up about 2½ in. (6.4 cm) of 3–8 mm beads and a 15 x 30 mm oval gemstone alternating with 11ºs or 15ºs. Sew through an A in a peyote ring, and sew back through the beads just strung. Pick up a 15º, and sew through the 11º in the bezeled coin. Retrace the thread path through the connection a few times, and end the thread.

[4] Add 12–18 in. (30–40 cm) of doubled Fireline to the peyote ring, exiting an A opposite the previous connection. Starting and ending with a 15º, pick up 2 in. (5 cm) of 3–8 mm beads and a 15 x 30 mm oval gemstone alternating with 15ºs. Starting and ending with a 15º, pick up this exact same bead grouping in reverse order. Sew through an edge 11º on the other

bezeled coin. The two 15ºs in the middle of this 4-in. (10 cm) section mark the center of the necklace. Pick up a 15º, and retrace the thread path through the connection a couple of times, leaving about 1 mm of space between the two 15ºs at the center of the necklace. This is where you will attach the focal and fringe. End the thread.

[5] Work as in steps 1–3 for the other side of the necklace, but switch the placement of the peyote ring and the bezeled coin.

Fringe

[1] On 1 yd. (.9 m) of Fireline, pick up 1½–2 in. (3.8–5 cm) of assorted beads ending with an 11º or 15º seed bead. Skip the 11º or 15º, and sew back through all the beads just added. Pick up the art-glass bead and a 6 mm bead, and loop the thread over the 1 mm space of exposed thread at the center of the necklace. Sew back through the 6 mm and art-glass bead.

[2] Using the same thread, work as in step 1 to add fringe as desired, keeping your tension loose so the fringe will drape. End the thread.

Garden
delight

**Stitch a floral profusion
and create a necklace
bursting with blooms**

designed by **Shirley Lim**

Living in Singapore, which is known as the Garden City, I am surrounded by flowers and greenery. I took inspiration from my surroundings and incorporated nature into this necklace design.

stepbystep

Flowers

[1] On 1 yd. (.9 m) of Fireline or thread, pick up five color H 11º seed beads, and tie them into a ring with a square knot (Basics), leaving a 12-in. (30 cm) tail. Sew through the first H again.

[2] Pick up an H, and sew through the next H (figure 1, a–b). Repeat around the ring, and step up (b–c).

[3] Using color A 11º seed beads, work a round in tubular peyote (Basics), and step up (figure 2, a–b).

[4] Pick up two As, and sew through the next A. Repeat around the ring, and step up through the first A added in the round (b–c).

[5] Pick up two color B 11º seed beads, and sew down through the next A and up through the following A (figure 3, a–b). Repeat around the ring, using the pairs of As added in the previous round as a base for tubular herringbone stitch (Basics), and step up (b–c).

[6] Using Bs, work two more rounds in tubular herringbone, and step up.

[7] Work an increase round: Pick up two color C 11º seed beads, sew down through the next B, pick up a C, and sew up through the following B (figure 4, a–b). Repeat to complete the round, and step up (b–c).

[8] Pick up a C, a color G 11º seed bead, and a C. Sew down through the next C, pick up two Cs, and sew up through the following C (c–d). Repeat to complete the round, and sew through the beadwork to exit an H in the first round (d–e).

[9] Pick up an H, sew through the center of the flower, and pick up an 8º seed bead, eight color I 11º seed beads, and three Gs. Sew back through the Is, the 8º, the H, and an H in the first round opposite the one your thread exited at the start of this step (photo). Sew back through the first round again to secure the new H. End the thread (Basics).

[10] Repeat steps 1–9, alternating through colors A, B, C, D, E, and F for the body of the flower, to make a total of 14 flowers for a necklace.

Necklace

Base

[1] On a comfortable length of Fireline or thread, pick up six color J 11º seed beads, and tie them into a ring with a square knot, leaving an 8-in. (20 cm) tail. Sew through the first J again.

[2] Using the ring as a base, work in tubular herringbone for about 1½ in. (3.8 cm).

MATERIALS

necklace 16 in. (41 cm)
- 14 8º seed beads
- 11º seed beads
  - 3–5 g in each of **6** colors: A, B, C, D, E, F
  - 1 g color G
  - 5–7 g color H
  - 1–2 g color I
  - 12–15 g color J
  - 10–14 g color K
- Fireline 6 lb. test, or nylon beading thread in a color to match the beads
- beading needles, #12

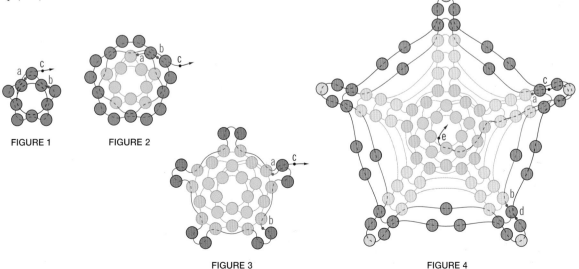

FIGURE 1

FIGURE 2

FIGURE 3

FIGURE 4

[3] Add fringe: With your thread exiting down a column, pick up 15 color K 11º seed beads and an H. Skip the H, and sew back through the next three Ks (**figure 5, a–b**). To add a branch, pick up three Ks and an H, skip the H, and sew back through the three Ks just added and the next three Ks (**b–c**). Repeat to add three more branches, and exit the first K added (**c–d**). Sew up through the next J, and work five rounds of herringbone, ending and adding thread (Basics) as needed.

[4] Repeat step 3 three times to add three more fringes.

[5] Add a flower: With your thread exiting a down column, pick up seven Hs, skip the last H added, and sew through the next one (**figure 6, a–b**). Pick up four Hs, skip four Hs, and sew through the first H added (**b–c**). This makes a leaf. Pick up two Hs and the center H in the base of a flower, and

sew back through the two Hs just added (**c–d**). Make a second leaf (**d–e**), and sew up through the next J.

[6] Work five rounds of herringbone, and add a fringe as in step 3. Repeat. Work five rounds of herringbone, and add a flower as in step 5.

[7] Repeat step 6.

[8] Work three rounds of herringbone, and add a fringe. Repeat twice. Work three rounds of herringbone, and add a flower. Repeat this sequence seven times.

[9] Repeat step 6 three times.

[10] Work five rounds of herringbone, and add a fringe. Repeat three times. Work in tubular herringbone for about 1½ in. (3.8 cm).

[11] To adjust the length of your necklace, add or remove rounds of herringbone on both ends of the necklace, taking care to keep the placement of the embellishments symmetrical.

Clasp

[1] Thread a needle on the tail. Pick up a J, and sew through the next two Js. Repeat twice, and step up through the first J added. Sew through all three Js just added to bring them together.

[2] Sew through the H in the center of a flower base, the J your thread just exited, and the next J. Continue around to connect the H in the flower base to all three Js at the end of the necklace, and end the thread.

[3] With your working thread, repeat step 1.

[4] Pick up enough Js to form a loop around the flower (about 31 Js). Sew back through the first J added, and continue through the J your thread exited and the next J. Retrace the thread path, connecting the loop to all three Js in the necklace base. End the thread.

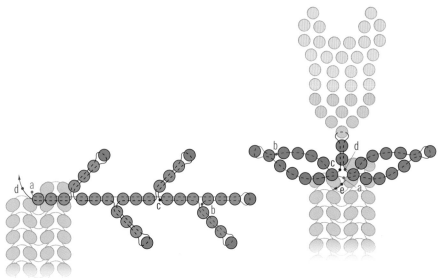

FIGURE 5   FIGURE 6

Chained
melody

Create a harmonious balance with linked loops and assorted chain

designed by **Jessica Fehrmann**

a

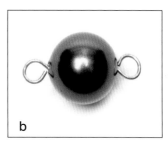

b

Link large rings into a chain by connecting them with pearls. Add casual, funky flair with longer lengths of chain and a handful of beads from your stash.

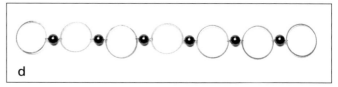

c

d

stepbystep

Bead components

[1] To make a dangle on a head pin, string a 9–12 mm glass pearl or bead, and make a plain loop (Basics and **photo a**). Repeat with the remaining 9–12 mms.

[2] To make a pearl connector, string an 8 mm freshwater or glass pearl or bead on an eye pin; make a plain loop (**photo b**). Repeat with the remaining 8 mms.

Assembly

[1] To create the chain of solid rings, open a loop (Basics) of a pearl connector, and attach a 25–30 mm solid ring. Close the loop. Open the remaining loop of the connector, and attach a second solid ring. Close loop (**photo c**).

[2] Open a loop of a connector, and attach the last solid ring added in the previous step. Close the loop. Open the remaining loop of the connector, attach a new solid ring, and close the loop. Repeat four times to connect

a total of seven solid rings with six connectors (**photo d**).

[3] Cut an 18-in. (46 cm) piece of large-link chain. Open a jump ring (Basics), and attach an end link of chain and an end solid ring. Close the jump ring.

[4] Cut a 17½-in. (44.5 cm) piece of medium-link chain. Open a jump ring, and attach an end link of chain and the same end solid ring from the previous step. Close the jump ring.

[5] Cut a 15½-in. (39.4 cm) piece of small-link chain. Open a jump ring, and attach an end link of chain and the same end solid ring from the previous steps. Close the jump ring.

[6] Cut a 33½-in. (85.1 cm) piece of extra-small-link chain. Fold the chain so one end is 14¾ in. (37.5 cm) and the other end is 18¾ in. (47.6 cm). Open a jump ring, and attach the link of chain at the fold and the same end solid ring from the previous steps. Close the jump ring (**photo e**).

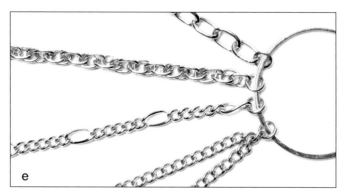

e

MATERIALS

necklace 29 in. (74 cm)

- **8–12** 9–12 mm assorted glass pearls or beads
- **6** 8 mm freshwater or glass pearls or beads
- **9** 25–30 mm solid rings
- lobster claw clasp
- chain in **4** varieties:
  18 in. (46 cm) large link (6 mm or 16 mm bar)
  17½ in. (44.5 cm) medium link (4–6 mm)
  15½ in. (39.4 cm) small link (3–4 mm)
  40½ in. (1 m) extra-small link (2–3 mm)
- **8–12** 1-in. (2.5 cm) head pins
- **6** 1½-in. (3.8 cm) eye pins
- **14–18** 3–4 mm jump rings
- chainnose pliers
- roundnose pliers
- wire cutters

f

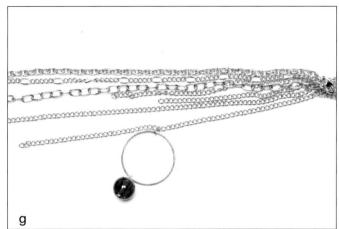

g

h

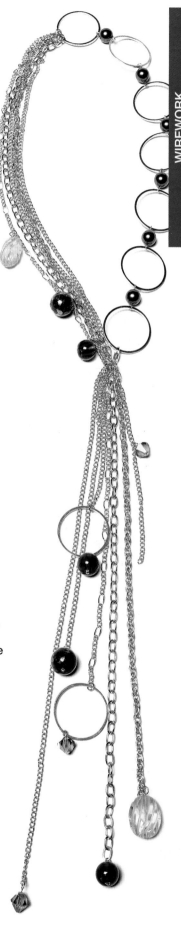

DESIGN NOTE:
• You can use almost any type of large ring to make this necklace. Try different textures, such as twisted or hammered; different finishes, such as polished or brushed; different shapes, such as oval; or different types of metal, such as copper, brass, or silver.

[7] Cut a 7-in. (18 cm) piece of extra-small-link chain, and fold it so one end is 3 in. (7.6 cm) and the other end is 4 in. (10 cm). Open a jump ring, and attach the link of chain at the fold and a lobster claw clasp. Identify a link in each of the chains added in steps 3–6 that is about 9 in. (23 cm) from the end ring. Slide each link onto the open jump ring, and close the jump ring **(photo f)**. The chains dangling below the lobster claw clasp will be referred to as the tassel.

[8] Open a jump ring, and attach a solid ring and a link of chain in the tassel of the necklace. Close the jump ring. Open the loop of a dangle, and attach it to the solid ring. Close the loop **(photo g)**. Repeat with the remaining solid ring, attaching it to a different chain.

[9] Open the loop of a dangle, and attach a link of chain. Close the jump ring **(photo h)**. Repeat with the remaining dangles, spacing them as desired. Note the three dangles along the neckline and the remaining dangles on the tassel in the photo on this page.

For a slightly different look, attach the dangles to the ends of the chains.

Curly cue

Coiled components add texture to a strung necklace

designed by **Kimberly Berlin**

MATERIALS

necklace 19 in. (48 cm)

- **13** 10 mm gemstone beads or pearls
- **24** 8 mm beads to match the 10 mms
- **14** 6 mm large-hole copper beads, gemstones, or pearls
- **22** 3 mm beads to match the 6 mms

- clasp
- 7 ft. (2.1 m) 16-gauge round copper or silver wire, half-hard
- 4 crimp beads
- 4 crimp covers
- flexible beading wire, .019
- chainnose pliers

- crimping pliers
- wire cutters
- 5 mm mandrel
- metal file or wire rounder
- pencil
- ruler

Bring out the best in your favorite chunky beads when you pair them with coiled wire. Using beads in graduated sizes adds to the flow of this necklace. The coiled components make elegant earrings, too.

stepbystep

Necklace

[1] Cut a 12-in. (30 cm) piece of 16-gauge wire, and file the ends or use a wire rounder to smooth them. Coil the wire around the 5 mm mandrel, keeping the coils straight and snugging them tight against each other, but not too tight around the mandrel. Using chainnose pliers, flatten the ends against the mandrel. Slide the coil off the mandrel.

[2] Using chainnose pliers, gently bend an end coil perpendicular to the remaining coils. Repeat on the other end, making sure the end coils are parallel **(photo a)**.

[3] Gently stretch the coils apart so the coil unit measures 1¾ in. (4.4 cm) from end to end **(photo b)**. If needed, use chainnose pliers to neaten the coils.

[4] Wrap the coil unit around the pencil to form a U shape **(photo c)**.

[5] Repeat steps 1–4 to make a total of seven coil units.

[6] Cut a 24-in. (61 cm) piece of beading wire. Center a coil unit with a 10 mm gemstone bead or pearl sandwiched between the ends **(photo d)**.

[7] On each end, string a 6 mm large-hole copper bead or gemstone or pearl, a 10 mm, a 6 mm, and a coil unit with a 10 mm sandwiched between the ends. Repeat twice, and string a 6 mm.

[8] On each end, string an alternating pattern of an 8 mm gemstone bead or pearl and a 3 mm large-hole copper bead or gemstone or pearl to the desired length.

[9] Test the fit, and add or remove beads as needed.

[10] On each end, string two crimp beads and half of the clasp. Go back through the crimp beads, crimp the crimp beads (Basics), and trim the tails. Close a crimp cover over each crimp.

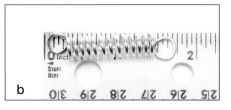

a

b

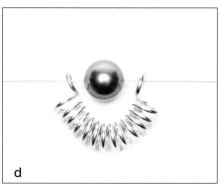

d

c

DESIGN NOTE:
If the end coils are not parallel, use pliers to tighten the coil until the ends are aligned. Take care not to change the shape of the coiled piece.

Raining petals

Beaded dangles evoke the gentle dropping of petals from a blossoming tree

designed by **Kat West**

MATERIALS

necklace 21½ in. (54.6 cm)

- **32** 10–12 mm oval gemstone beads
- **5–7** 10 mm gemstone rondelles
- **200–212** assorted accent beads, including: 8 mm round crystals, 4–6 mm freshwater pearls, 4 mm bicone crystals, 4 mm round crystals, 2–4 mm semi-precious beads, 6º seed beads, 8º seed beads, 11º seed beads, and 11º cylinder beads
- **3** Y-shaped connectors with loops (Pacific Silverworks, pacificsilverworks.com)
- **2** S-hook clasps
- **2 or more** 5 x 3 mm bead caps
- **6 in.** (15 cm) 20- or 22-gauge wire
- **6 ft.** (1.8 m) 24-gauge wire
- **42–48** 2-in. (5 cm) head pins, variety of plain and single- and triple-ball decorative heads
- **11** 7 mm twisted oval jump rings, 16-gauge
- **4** 6 mm soldered jump rings
- chainnose pliers
- roundnose pliers
- wire cutters

stepbystep

Centerpiece

The centerpiece is made up of one large and two small Y-shaped connectors.
[1] To make a simple dangle, string the beads of your choice on a head pin, and make the first half of a wrapped loop (Basics). Attach the dangle to a side loop of a connector, and complete the wraps **(photo a)**. Repeat to add dangles to the other side loops of the connectors as desired. If your small connectors have large central loops, like those shown here, you may wish to attach two or more dangles **(photo b)**.
[2] For extra movement, make jointed dangles for the large connector's central loop: Cut a 3-in. (7.6 cm) piece of 24-gauge wire, and make the first half of a wrapped loop. Attach the central loop or an oval jump ring, and complete the wraps. String your choice of beads and bead caps, and make the first half of a wrapped loop. Make a simple dangle as in step 1, attach it to the unfinished loop, and complete the wraps.

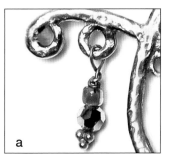

a

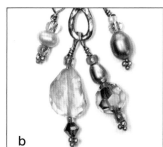

b

c

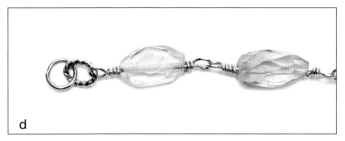

d

e

f

If you attached the jointed dangle to a jump ring, open the jump ring (Basics), attach it to the central loop, and close the jump ring.

Repeat to add jointed dangles to the central loop as desired (photo c).

[3] Open an oval jump ring, attach an end loop of the large and a small connector, and close the jump ring. Repeat to attach the remaining small connector to the large connector.

[4] If desired, begin a simple dangle, attach it to a jump ring between connectors, and complete the wraps. Repeat on the other side.

Chain

[1] Cut a 4-in. (10 cm) piece of 24-gauge wire, and make a wrapped loop. String a 10–12 mm oval gemstone bead, and make the first half of a wrapped loop on the other end. Attach the unfinished loop to the end loop of a small connector, and complete the wraps.

[2] Repeat step 1 seven times, but attach each new gemstone link to the end loop of the previous link.

[3] Open an oval jump ring, attach a soldered jump ring and the remaining loop of the last gemstone link, and close the jump ring (photo d).

[4] Begin several simple dangles as in step 1 of "Centerpiece," attach them to the loops of the gemstone links, and complete the wraps (photo e).

[5] Repeat steps 1–4 to make the other side of the necklace.

Clasp bar

[1] Cut a 6-in. (15 cm) piece of 20- or 22-gauge wire, depending upon which gauge wire fits through your rondelles. Make the first half of a wrapped loop, attach a soldered jump ring, and complete the wraps.

[2] String a bead cap, a 10 mm rondelle, an 8° seed bead, a rondelle, an 8°, a rondelle, and a bead cap.

[3] Make the first half of a wrapped loop, attach a soldered jump ring, and complete the wraps.

[4] Attach an S-hook to each soldered jump ring.

[5] If you wish, make several simple dangles, and use oval jump rings to attach them to the end loops of the clasp bar (photo f).

EDITOR'S NOTE:
If you can't find the exact Y-shaped connectors shown in this project, try another source, such as Fire Mountain Gems and Beads (firemountaingems.com).

Modest exhibition

Use a minimalist approach to feature a brilliant gem in a graceful wire setting

designed by
Lilian Chen

stepbystep

Pendant bezel and bail

[1] Cut a 7-in. (18 cm) piece of 22-gauge square wire, and use roundnose pliers to make a small hook at one end. Use your fingers and chainnose pliers to form a small spiral around the hook (photo a). This spiral will sit against the front of the gemstone.

[2] Position the spiral as you would like it placed against the stone. Without bending the wire, rock the wire back so it is flat against the back of the stone and the spiral is

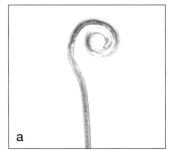

a

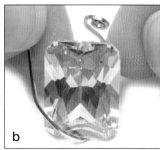

b

pointing up. Hold the wire tight against the back of the stone, and bend the wire up and around the bottom edge of the stone so that you cross the corner opposite the starting spiral (photo b).

[3] Pull the wire around the back of the stone to the

starting point, and cross the wire in front of the spiral end, just behind the top edge of the stone. Fold the spiral down over the wire and the top edge of the stone, so it sits securely on the front (photo c).

[4] Bend the wire back over

c

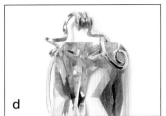

d

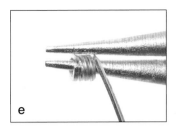

e

f

g

h

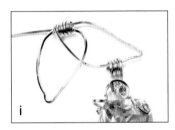

i

j

k

the spiral and the top of the stone. Use roundnose pliers and your fingers to coil and curve the wire over the top of the stone. Trim the wire as needed, and use roundnose pliers to make a small hook at the end. Secure the hook to the wire along the edge of the stone (photo d).

[5] To make a bail, cut a 2-in. (5 cm) piece of 22-gauge square wire, and make a four-wrap coil at the end using roundnose pliers. Because the pliers are tapered, you'll need to adjust the position of the wire with each turn so the coils are consistent in size (photo e).

[6] Bend the wire down from the coil, and begin curving the wire back up. Attach the pendant to the hook (photo f), and finish with a decorative spiral.

[7] On a head pin, string a 10 mm pearl, and make the first half of a wrapped loop (Basics). Attach the dangle to the bottom of the pendant, and complete the wraps (photo g).

Leaf connector

[1] Cut a 10-in. (25 cm) piece of 22-gauge square wire, and make a four-wrap coil at one end, as in step 5 of "Pendant bezel and bail."

[2] Holding the coil with the long tail on the left, bring the wire down under the coil to the right. Shape the wire into a curve with your fingers, and make an upward bend about 1 in. (2.5 cm) from the coil, using your pliers as needed. Slide the bail onto the wire, so the front of the pendant is facing you, and feed the end of the wire through the coil made in step 1. Gently pull the wire through the coil, shaping the loop into a leaf shape

(photo h). Keep in mind that this segment will hold both the pendant and part of the necklace chain.

[3] To make the second leaf segment, curve the wire exiting the coil downward, and make a U-shaped bend about ¾ in. (1.9 cm) from the coil. Feed the wire through the coil, shaping the segment into a leaf as you pull (photo i).

[4] Bend the wire up, away from the coil. Make a U-shaped bend about 1 in. (2.5 cm) from the coil, and feed the wire through the coil, creating the third leaf shape (photo j). Keep in mind that this leaf will hold part of the necklace chain.

[5] Bend the wire up, under the third leaf, and curve the end into a spiral (photo k). Use your fingers to gently shape the connector as desired.

Assembly

[1] Determine the finished length of your necklace,

subtract 1 in. (2.5 cm), and cut two pieces of chain to this length. These pieces will form the long side of the necklace.

[2] Measure the length of your leaf connector, and multiply this length by two. Subtract this length from the chain length determined in step 1, and cut two pieces of chain to the new length for the short side of the necklace. (In my necklace, the long chains were 15 in./38 cm, and the leaf connector was 1½ in./3.8 cm long, so the short chains were 12 in./30 cm each.)

[3] Cut a 2-in. (5 cm) piece of 24-gauge wire, and make the first half of a wrapped loop. Attach an end link of each long chain, and pass the chains through the first leaf of the connector. Be careful not to go through the pendant bail or twist the chains. Attach the remaining end links to the loop, and complete the wraps.

[4] String a 3 mm accent

bead, and make the first half of a wrapped loop. Attach half of the clasp, and complete the wraps.

[5] Repeat steps 3 and 4 with the short chains, passing through the third leaf of the connector instead of the first.

MATERIALS

necklace 16 in. (41 cm)

- 12 x 15 mm gemstone or cubic zirconia, undrilled
- 10 mm pearl
- 2 3 mm accent beads
- clasp
- 19 in. (48 cm) 22-gauge square wire, half-hard
- 4 in. (10 cm) 24-gauge wire, half-hard
- 1½ yd. (1.4 m) cable chain, 2–3 mm links
- 1½-in. (3.8 cm) head pin
- chainnose pliers
- roundnose pliers
- wire cutters

Beaded
clusters

Twist an
assortment of
beads into an
organic necklace

designed by **Jean Ann Reeves**

MATERIALS

necklace 20 in. (51 cm)
- **140–180** 4–10 mm assorted glass beads, crystals, and pearls
- 5–7 g 6º seed beads
- 5–7 g 8º seed beads
- 5–7 g 11º seed beads
- toggle clasp
- 6½ yd. (5.9 m) 24-gauge wire
- **4** crimp beads
- **4** crimp covers (optional)
- flexible beading wire, .018–.020
- chainnose pliers
- crimping pliers
- roundnose pliers
- wire cutters

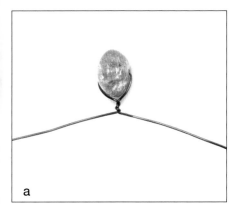

a

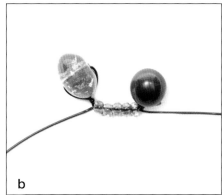

b

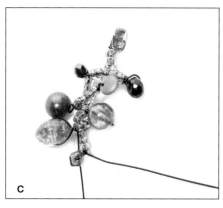

c

d

e

f

Create a bead soup with beads in pleasing shapes, sizes, and colors for a necklace that displays beauty and variety. Choose craft wire in a color that coordinates with the beads, or use a precious-metal wire that will stand out.

stepbystep

Focal cluster

[1] Cut a 5-ft. (1.5 m) piece of 24-gauge wire, and fold it in half. String a 4–10 mm bead, and twist the wire together three times (**photo a**).

[2] On one side, string three to seven 6º, 8º, and/or 11º seed beads and a 4–10 mm bead. Twist the wire around the base of the 4–10 mm bead (**photo b**).

[3] Repeat step 2 seven times for a total of eight units.

[4] Fold the beaded portion of wire in half, and twist the beaded wire together to form a cluster. Bend the larger beads to one surface to create the front of the necklace. This allows the seed beads to serve as the background support structure (**photo c**).

[5] Weave the unbeaded wire through the bead cluster to exit the opposite end, and repeat steps 2–4.

[6] Twist the unbeaded wire ends around beads in both clusters to

hold the clusters together (**photo d**).

[7] On one wire, repeat steps 2–4. Weave the working wire around the beads in the new cluster and the previous cluster to connect the clusters together (**photo e**). Repeat to the end of the wire, and weave the tail into the beadwork.

[8] Repeat step 7 on the remaining wire.

[9] Cut a 5-ft. (1.5 m) piece of 24-gauge wire, and weave one end into the beadwork to anchor the wire. Continue adding bead clusters as before.

[10] Repeat step 9 on the other side of the beadwork. If needed, continue cutting new wire and adding bead clusters on alternating sides of the original cluster until the bead clusters measure about 6 in. (15 cm) or your desired length.

Bridging clusters

[1] Cut an 18-in. (46 cm) piece of 24-gauge wire, and fold it in half. String it through an end loop of the focal cluster, and twist the wire together (**photo f**).

[2] On each half of the wire, make five to seven units as in steps 2 and 3 of "Focal cluster." Twist the beaded units together (**photo g**). Bend the large beads to the front of the necklace.

[3] Repeat steps 1 and 2 on the remaining end of the focal cluster.

[4] Cut a 20-in. (51 cm) piece of 24-gauge wire to reinforce the structure of the necklace. Leaving a 2-in. (5 cm) tail, weave the wire through the bead clusters from one end of the necklace to the other. Add beads to conceal the wire as desired.

[5] On one end, twist the tails of the beaded clusters and the reinforcing wire together (**photo h**). With all three wires twisted together, make a plain or wrapped loop (Basics). Repeat on the other end.

Assembly

[1] Cut an 8-in. (20 cm) piece of beading wire. String a crimp bead, six 11º seed beads, and the loop of

DESIGN NOTE:
String your beads in a random order for an organic look.

Use dark craft wire with moody shades for an evening look.

g

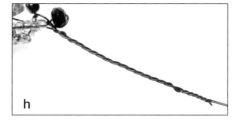

h

a bridging cluster. Go back through the crimp bead, and crimp it (Basics).
[2] Determine the final length of your necklace, and subtract the length of the clasp and focal and bridging clusters. Divide the remainder in two, and string assorted 4–10 mms and seed beads to that length.
[3] String a crimp bead and half of the clasp. Go back through the crimp bead and the next few beads. Crimp the crimp bead, and trim the wire. If desired, close a crimp cover over each crimp with chainnose pliers.
[4] Repeat steps 1–3 on the remaining end.

Sew
wired

Use twisted wire to sew five antique shell buttons into a necklace

designed by **Wendy Witchner**

These five mismatched mother-of-pearl buttons grouped together with oxidized silver create an antique look. Try this design with any combination of four- or two-hole buttons and wire — for instance, ceramic and colored craft wire, Lucite and copper, or Czech glass and gold — to achieve a funky, casual, or sophisticated necklace.

stepbystep

Wire components

[1] Cut a 4½-in. (11.4 cm) piece of 18-gauge twisted wire, and use round-nose pliers and your fingers to form a loose spiral about ⅞ in. (2.2 cm) in diameter, curving the tail close to the outer edge of the spiral. Place the loose spiral on an anvil, and hammer it a few times, flattening the raised surface (photo a). Repeat three times to make a total of four loose spirals.

[2] To make an end component, cut a 4¼-in. (10.8 cm) piece of 18-gauge twisted wire, and use roundnose pliers and your fingers to form a tight spiral about ⁹⁄₁₆ in. (1.4 cm) in diameter, leaving a ½-in. (1.3 cm) tail. Using roundnose pliers, turn the tail up, and make a small perpendicular hook (photo b). Hammer the spiral part of the end component.

[3] To make a hook component, cut a 1½-in. (3.8 cm) piece of 22-gauge round wire. Using roundnose pliers, turn up one end, and squeeze it to the wire to make a small hook (photo c). Bend the wire to make a larger hook, curving it in toward the small hook, and back out again. Make a medium-sized hook at the other end (photo d). Hammer the hook component.

Buttons

[1] Cut a 4¼-in. (10.8 cm) piece of 22-gauge twisted wire. Bend the wire about 1¼ in. (3.2 cm) from one end, and string two diagonal holes of a four-hole button on both ends of the wire with the top of the button facing the bend in the wire (photo e).

[2] Using the long end of the wire, go through an adjacent hole (photo f). Cross the working end of the wire over the previous wire, and go through the remaining hole.

[3] Position the tail and the working wire on each side of the button. Using

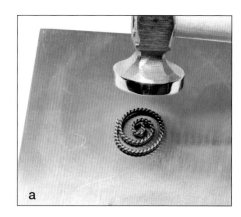
a

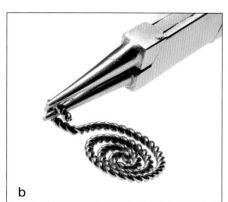
b

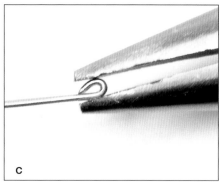
c

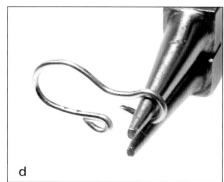
d

e

f

DESIGN NOTES:
• Twisted wire might mar the planishing surface of your hammer. To avoid ruining a smooth hammer, use a hammer that you don't mind roughing up a bit, use a rawhide or rubber mallet, skip the second half of step 1, or use round instead of twisted wire to make the spirals.
• This piece uses wire that was already oxidized. To speed up the oxidation process, you can submerge the components in liver of sulfur, following the manufacturer's instructions. Then polish the surface of the wire to bring out the shine on the raised parts.

roundnose pliers, turn up the end of the tail to make a simple loop (photo g). Trim the working wire if needed, and repeat with the other wire end to make a second simple loop.

[4] Repeat steps 1–3 three times to make a total of four four-hole button units.

[5] Cut a 2½-in. (6.4 cm) piece of 22-gauge twisted wire. Bend the wire in half, and string both holes of a two-hole button on both ends of the wire with the top of the button facing the bend in the wire. Position the ends of the wire on each side of the button, and turn a simple loop on each end.

Assembly

[1] To connect a button component to a loose spiral, gently pull the tail of a loose spiral away from the spiral, and string the plain loop of a button component (photo h). Slide the spiral around to position the spiral tail at the bottom, and string a plain loop of another button component. Position the button components opposite each other, and press the tail close to the spiral (photo i).

[2] Connect the remaining button components and spirals, placing the two-hole button in the center of the necklace.

[3] Cut a 6½-in. (16.5 cm) piece of chain in half. Open the remaining plain loop (Basics) on an end button component, and attach an end link of the chain. Close the loop (photo j). Repeat on the other side.

[4] Open the hook on the end spiral component, and attach an end link of a chain. Close the loop (photo k). Repeat with the hook component on the other side.

MATERIALS

necklace 18 in. (46 cm)
- 1 5/16-in. (3.3 cm) two-hole button
- 4 1 3/16-in. (3 cm) four-hole buttons
- 22¼ in. (56.5 cm) 18-gauge twisted wire
- 19½ in. (49.5 cm) 22-gauge twisted wire
- 1½ in. (3.8 cm) 22-gauge round wire
- 6½ in. (16.5 cm) chain
- anvil
- chasing hammer
- chainnose pliers
- roundnose pliers
- wire cutters

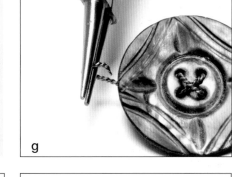

g

h

i

j

k

MATERIALS

necklace 18 in. (46 cm) with
3-in. (7.6 cm) dangle

- **12** 10–16 mm faceted
  gemstone briolettes or
  crystal drop beads
- **2** 4 mm beads
- 18 in. (46 cm) large-link circle
  chain (artbeads.com)
- **5–7** 24-in. (61 cm) lengths of
  small-link chain, various styles
  and finishes
- 34 in. (86 cm) 24- or
  26-gauge wire (choose the
  thickest gauge that will go
  through the holes of the
  briolettes or drops)
- clasp
- chainnose pliers
- roundnose pliers
- wire cutters

Chained reaction

Combine large- and small-link chain in mixed metals with wire-wrapped briolettes for an up-to-date delight

designed by **Angela Casaccio**

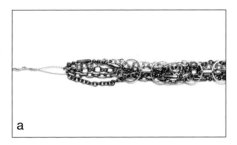

a

b

c

stepbystep

[1] Cut 2 in. (5 cm) of wire, fold it in half, and string an end link of each small-link chain. Twist the wire ends together to secure.

[2] Weave the wire through the links of the large-link chain, going up through the first link, down through the second link, up through the third link, and so on, pulling the bundle of small-link chains all the way through the large-link chain. Stop when the bundle of chains extends about ½–1 in. (1.3–2.5 cm) beyond the large-link chain (**photo a**). Remove the wire.

[3] Trim the other end of the small-link chains so they also extend about ½–1 in. (1.3–2.5 cm) beyond the large-link chain.

[4] Cut 3 in. (7.6 cm) of wire, and make the first half of a wrapped loop (Basics). On one end of the necklace, slide the end link of the large-link chain into the loop. Slide a link of each small-link chain into the loop, allowing the ½–1-in. (1.3–2.5 cm) ends to dangle (**photo b**). Complete the wraps. String a 4 mm bead on the wire, and make the first half of a wrapped loop. Attach half of the clasp, and complete the wraps (**photo c**).

[5] Repeat step 4 on the other end of the necklace, attaching the other half of the clasp.

[6] Select five chain segments left over from step 3, and cut them so they vary

d

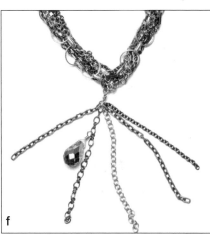

e

f

from 2–3 in. (5–7.6 cm) in length. Cut 2 in. (5 cm) of wire, make the first half of a wrapped loop, slide an end link of each chain segment into the loop, and complete the wraps. Make the first half of a wrapped loop at the other end of the wire, attach it to a couple of chains at the middle of the necklace, and complete the wraps (**photo d**).

[7] Cut 2 in. (5 cm) of wire, and string a 10–16 mm briolette or drop bead. Make a set of wraps as for a top-drilled bead (Basics). Make the first half of a wrapped loop with the remaining wire (**photo e**), attach it to any link on a chain in the dangle, and complete the wraps (**photo f**).

[8] Repeat step 7 with the remaining briolettes or drop beads, attaching them to the dangle and the center portion of the necklace as desired.

DESIGN NOTE:
Drape your necklace on a neckform or attach it to a Chain-Stā before attaching the briolettes or drop beads. It will be easier to see how the beads will fall if the necklace is hanging as it would be worn.

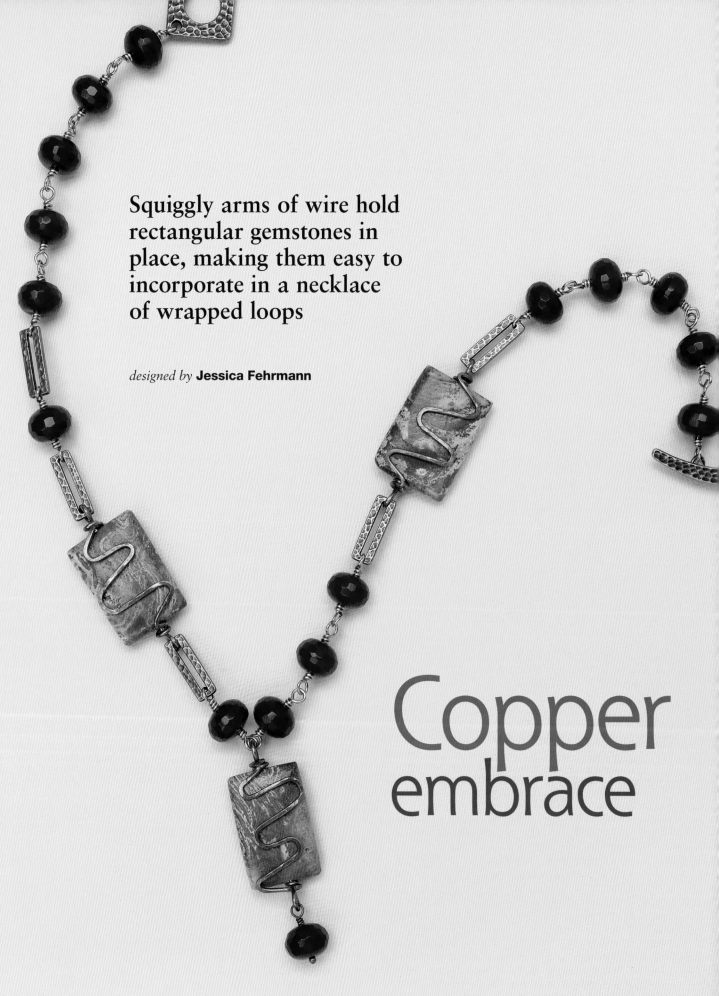

Squiggly arms of wire hold
rectangular gemstones in
place, making them easy to
incorporate in a necklace
of wrapped loops

designed by **Jessica Fehrmann**

Copper
embrace

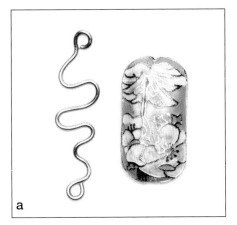

a

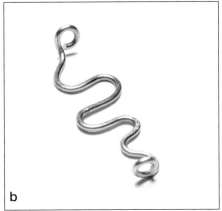

b

c

d

MATERIALS

necklace 19 in. (48 cm)

- **3** 20 x 30 mm rectangle beads (striped jasper)
- **16** 8 x 12 mm faceted glass rondelles (red)
- **5** 6 x 18 mm hammered rectangle links (by TierraCast)
- toggle clasp (by TierraCast)
- 42 in. (1.1 m) 16-gauge wire (copper)
- 45 in. (1.2 m) 20-gauge wire (copper)
- 1½-in. (3.8 cm) head pin (copper)
- 5–6 mm jump ring (copper)
- anvil or bench block
- hammer
- chainnose pliers
- roundnose pliers
- wire cutters

stepbystep

Squiggle links and pendant

[1] Cut a 5-in. (13 cm) piece of 6-gauge wire, and make a plain loop (Basics).
[2] Using roundnose pliers, grasp the wire ¼ in. (6 mm) below the plain loop. Pull both ends of the wire around the pliers, making a U-shaped turn in the same plane as the loop.
[3] Continue making U-turns to create a squiggle, making sure it is no wider than the 20 x 30 mm rectangle beads. When your squiggle is the same length as the bead (not counting the plain loop made in step 1), trim the wire to ½ in. (1.3 cm), and make another plain loop (photo a). Adjust the loops so they align with the holes of the rectangle bead.
[4] Repeat steps 1–3 to make a second squiggle component, but in step 3, make the squiggle 2–3 mm longer.
[5] Place a squiggle component on an anvil or bench block, and hammer both

sides of the squiggle. Do not hammer the plain loops. Hammer the other squiggle component.
[6] Using chainnose pliers, grasp a plain loop on a squiggle component, and bend it perpendicular to the squiggle. Repeat with the other plain loop, bending it parallel to the first (photo b). Repeat to bend the loops of the other squiggle component.
[7] Place the squiggle component from step 3 on a rectangle bead (you might need to adjust the squiggle).
[8] Holding the shorter squiggle component against one side of the rectangle bead, place the longer squiggle component on the other side.
[9] Cut a 4-in. (10 cm) piece of 16-gauge wire, and make a plain loop on one end. String the longer squiggle, the shorter squiggle, and a rectangle bead. Position one squiggle on each side of the rectangle bead, then string the remaining loops of the squiggles. Trim

the wire to ½ in. (1.3 cm), and make a plain loop (photo c). Repeat step 1–9 to make a total of three squiggle links.
[10] On a head pin, string an 8 x 12 mm rondelle, and make the first half of a wrapped loop (Basics). Attach a plain loop of a squiggle link, and complete the wraps (photo d).

Assembly

[1] Cut a 3-in. (7.6 cm) piece of 20-gauge wire, string a rondelle, and make a wrapped loop (Basics) on each end, attaching the adjacent components before completing the wraps. Attach rondelle links, squiggle links, and rectangle links as shown in the photo.
[2] Use a jump ring (Basics) to attach half of a clasp to each end.

Rosy posy pendant

Use a round loom
to bring a wire
flower into bloom

designed by **Sharilyn Miller**

I'm often inspired by the designs found in nature — the shapes and textures of flowers, leaves, and land formations. Sometimes, an idea will come to me from a very unexpected source, and it will result in a beautiful pendant.

stepbystep

Flower pendant
Weaving the posy

[1] Clean all of your wire with 0000 steel wool.

[2] On a 2-in. (5 cm) head pin, string a 3–4 mm bead, and make a wrapped loop (Basics). Repeat to make a total of 12 dangles, using assorted beads as desired. Set them aside.

[3] Use permanent marker to number the flower loom pegs from 1 to 12, counter-clockwise (photo a).

[4] Cut 4 yd. (3.7 m) of 22-gauge wire, and wrap one end around the holding peg, leaving a short tail.

[5] Bring the wire between pegs 1 and 12, cross the loom, and bring it between pegs 6 and 7.

[6] Wrap the wire around peg 6, and bring it back between pegs 1 and 12 (photo b).

[7] Wrap the wire around peg 12, cross the loom, and bring it between pegs 5 and 6 (photo c).

[8] Wrap the wire around peg 5, cross the loom, and bring it between pegs 11 and 12. Continue wrapping the pegs in a clockwise direction as described in steps 5–7 until every peg is wrapped. The wire should exit between pegs 1 and 12 (photo d).

[9] Repeat steps 5–8 twice, until all 12 pegs have been wrapped three times. When finished, wrap the remaining wire around the holding peg to keep it in place. Do not trim the wire tails (photo e).

Wrapping the center

[1] Cut 1 yd. (.9 m) of 24-gauge wire, and wrap one end around the holding peg, leaving a short tail.

[2] Bring the wire under the center of the loom, and, working from back to front, weave it up between the loops around pegs 6 and 7. String a dangle on the wire, then go down between the loops around pegs 12 and 1, pulling the wire firmly, but not too tight (photo f).

[3] Go up between the loops around 5 and 6; add a dangle, and go down between the loops around 11 and 12. Pull firmly. Continue crossing over the center of the flower, weaving between opposite sets of loops, until you've added six dangles. Once you've gone between each set of three loops, start weaving between each loop on each peg until you have gone through all 36 loops (photo g). Attach a total of 12 dangles by adding a

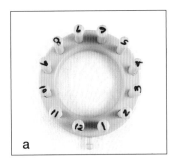

a

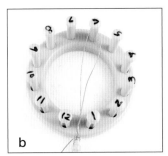

b

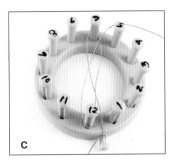

c

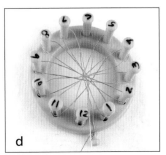

d

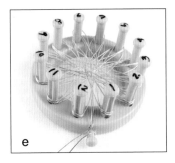

e

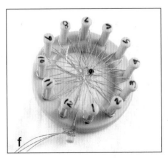

f

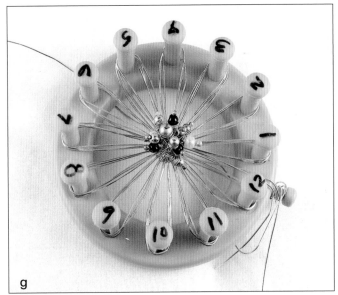

g

DESIGN NOTE:
The Knifty Knitter comes in several sizes. Use a loom with five pegs and one layer of wraps to make a smaller version of the pendant.

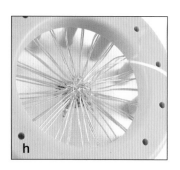

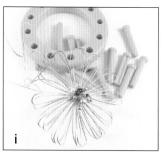

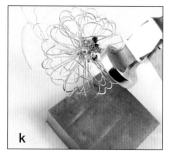

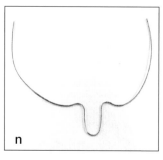

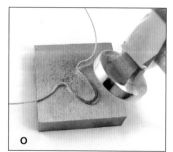

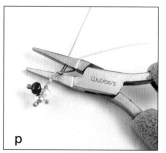

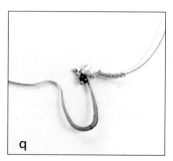

MATERIALS

necklace 15 in. (38 cm)
with 2¼-in. (5.7 cm)
diameter pendant

- **42** 3–4 mm assorted
  beads, pearls, or crystals
- dead-soft round wire
  12 in. (30 cm) 14-gauge
  neck wire
  24 in. (61 cm) 16-gauge
  wrapping wire
  4 yd. (3.7 m) 22-gauge
  1 yd. (.9 m) 24-gauge
- 10 in. (25 cm) chain
- 24-gauge head pins
  30 3-in. (7.6 cm)
  12 2-in. (5 cm)
- **2** 6 mm jump rings
- toggle bar
- chasing hammer
- Knifty Knitter flower loom
  (walmart.com)
- permanent marker
- steel bench block
- 0000 steel wool
- chainnose pliers
- flatnose pliers
- roundnose pliers
- heavy-duty wire cutters

EDITOR'S NOTE:
The flower loom kit
includes step-by-step
illustrations.

dangle whenever you weave
through a set of three loops.
Bring the wire through the
center, exiting the back of the
loom. Unwind the tail from
the holding peg and bring it
through the center, next to
the other wire **(photo h)**.
[4] Twist both ends of the
24-gauge wire together tightly.

Shaping
[1] Remove the pegs from
the loom **(photo i)**.
[2] Use the tips of a small
roundnose pliers to shape all
36 loops into petals **(photo j)**.
Each petal will be slightly
different, which is natural
for a flower.
[3] If desired, hammer each
petal on a steel bench block
very carefully with a chasing
hammer **(photo k)**. This will
keep the petals from being
easily bent out of shape.

Bail
[1] To make a bail on the
back of the flower pendant,
make a large wrapped loop
with the two 22-gauge wires
(photo l).
[2] Coil the longest 24-gauge
wire tightly around the loop,
covering it completely. Trim
all the wire ends when finished, spiral in their ends,
and set the flower pendant
aside **(photo m)**.

Neck wire
[1] Cut a 12-in. (30 cm)
piece of 14-gauge wire, and
at its center, use roundnose
pliers and your fingers to
form a U shape. Bend each
wire end out from the U
shape **(photo n)**.
[2] Hammer the U shape
with a chasing hammer to
harden it **(photo o)**. Set the
neck wire aside.
[3] String the remaining
pearls, beads, and crystals on
each of the 30 3-in. (7.6 cm)
head pins.

[4] Pick up three head pins, and twist them together tightly near the beads to create a bundle (photo p). Repeat with the remaining 27 head pins.

[5] Pick up one bundle, and wrap the wires tightly around the neck wire, starting near the U shape (photo q). Repeat four times to embellish one side of the necklace.

[6] String the flower pendant on the neck wire and center it (photo r). If desired, wrap the pendant in place with a scrap piece of 24-gauge wire to keep it from moving.

[7] Repeat step 5 on the opposite side of the neck wire, using the remaining beaded bundles (photo s).

[8] Create a large wrapped loop on one end of the neck wire (photo t). Make a decorative spiral on the other end of the neck wire (photo u), making sure the wire ends are relatively even in length from the center of the neck wire. Hammer if desired.

Finishing

[1] Cut a 10-in. (25 cm) piece of chain. Open a jump ring (Basics), and attach a toggle bar to one end of the chain.

[2] Open a jump ring, and attach the other end of the chain to the decorative spiral (photo v).

[3] Cut a 12-in. (30 cm) piece of 16-gauge wire, and make a spiral on one end. Starting on one side of the flower pendant, position the spiral between the first two wrapped bundles. Wrap the wire around the neck wire, placing the 16-gauge wire between the gaps in the bundles (photo w). Spiral the other end, and push it flat against the neck wire, near the wrapped loop. Repeat on the other side of the neck wire.

r

s

t

u

v

w

After wrapping the head pin bundles around the neck wire, decorative spirals can be created on each wire end.

Freeform
for all

A randomly winding
wire coil has an
abstract effect in this
beautiful asymmetrical
design

designed by **Leah Hanoud**

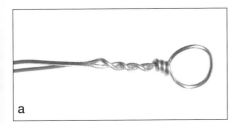

a

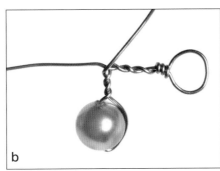

b

c

d

e

f

stepbystep

Necklace frame

[**1**] Cut a 4-ft. (1.2 m) piece of 24-gauge craft wire. At the center of the wire, make a wrapped loop (Basics), but do not trim the wrapping wire. Instead, bend the wrapping wire down to make it parallel to the other wire. Twist the wires together for ¼ in. (6 mm) to begin the twisted core of the necklace frame (**photo a**).

[**2**] On one wire, string a 6–8 mm bead, and slide it down to within ¼ in. (6 mm) of the core. Bend the wire around the bead and back toward the core. Holding the wire against the bead, twist the bead a few times. This creates a twisted branch connecting the bead to the core (**photo b**). Twist the wires together for ¼ in. (6 mm) to continue the core.

[**3**] Using the longer of the two wires, repeat step 2, positioning the new bead on the opposite side of the core as the previous bead (**photo c**). Repeat for the length of the necklace frame, keeping in mind the following:

• Gradually increase the size of the beads as you work toward the center of the necklace frame.

• To help the necklace lie properly when worn, add smaller beads to one side of the core and larger beads to the other side. When you add a large bead to one side of the core, you may need to add two or three smaller beads on the opposite side to balance it.

• As you work, curve the necklace frame so the smaller beads are on the inside of the curve and the larger beads are on the outside of the curve.

• When your wires get short, cut a new 4-ft. (1.2 m) piece of 24-gauge craft wire. Fold the wire in half, creating two parallel wires. Starting 1 in. (2.5 cm) back from where your previous wires ended, thread the new parallel wires between two branches so the core rests in the fold (**photo d**). Wrap the two new parallel wires around the core one at a time. Where the two previous wires end, begin twisting the two new wires together to continue the core (**photo e**). Using chainnose pliers, tuck the ends of the previous wires into the core.

• When your necklace frame is 7–8 in. (18–20 cm) long, gradually decrease the size of the beads, working the second half of the necklace frame as a mirror image of the first. Reserve two 6–8 mm beads for "Clasp."

[**4**] Make a wrapped loop, and trim the excess wire. Bend the twisted branches to create the desired look.

Coil embellishment

[**1**] Cut a 4-ft. (1.2 m) piece of 24-gauge craft wire. Wrap one end around the wraps of the wrapped loop on one end of the necklace frame (**photo f**).

g

[**2**] Cut a piece of 24-gauge craft wire to a length appropriate for the coiling tool you're using, and coil the wire on a 2 mm mandrel. Remove the coil from the mandrel.

[**3**] Slide the coil onto the wire added in step 1. Wrap the coil around the beads as desired (**photo g**) until you run out of coil. Wrap the wire from step 1 once or twice around the core where the coil ends.

[4] Repeat steps 2 and 3 until you reach the other end of the necklace frame. Wrap the end of the wire around the wraps of the wrapped loop, and trim the excess wire.

Clasp

[1] Cut an 18-in. (46 cm) piece of 24-gauge craft wire, and use the coiling tool and 2 mm mandrel to make a 1-in. (2.5 cm) coil.

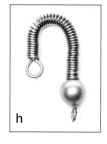

[2] Cut a 2-in. (5 cm) piece of 18-gauge wire. Make a plain loop (Basics) on one end. String a 6–8 mm bead and the 1-in. (2.5 cm) coil, and make another plain loop perpendicular to the first. Curve the coil into a hook clasp **(photo h)**.

[3] Open a 6 mm jump ring (Basics), and attach the loop of the hook clasp just below the 6–8 mm bead and the wrapped loop on one end of the necklace frame.

DESIGN NOTES:
• When you reserve two 6–8 mm beads in "Necklace frame" step 3, test to make sure that one of the beads' holes will accommodate the 18-gauge wire you'll use for the clasp.
• Try using colored craft wire to give your necklace an extra pop of color.

[4] Cut a 2½-in. (6.4 cm) piece of chain. Open a jump ring, and attach an end link of the chain and the wrapped loop on the other end of the necklace frame.

[5] On a head pin, string a 6–8 mm bead, and make the first half of a wrapped loop. Slide the remaining end link of chain into the loop, and complete the wraps.

MATERIALS

necklace 15–17 in. (38–43 cm)
• **5** 20 mm round gemstone beads
• **6** 16 mm round gemstone beads
• **10–12** 12 mm round gemstone, crystal pearl, or wood beads
• **14** 10 mm round gemstone, crystal pearl, or wood beads
• **12–16** 10 mm faceted gemstone lentil beads or coin pearls
• **8** 8 x 14 mm faceted gemstone rondelles, or a mixture of **15–20** 8 mm round gemstone beads and **15–20** 6 mm round crystal pearls
• **20–40** 8 mm faceted gemstone rondelles or button pearls
• 2 in. (5 cm) 18-gauge wire
• spool of 24-gauge craft wire
• 2½ in. (6.4 cm) chain, 15–17 mm links
• 1½-in. (3.8 cm) head pin
• **2** 6 mm jump rings
• coiling tool with 2 mm round mandrel, such as the Twist 'n' Curl or Coiling Gizmo
• chainnose pliers
• roundnose pliers
• wire cutters

A coiled clasp continues the necklace design.

Contributors

Mark Avery has been a jewelry designer and bead maker for 15 years. Mark enjoys coming up with new ways to make beads in his studio in Lansing, N.Y.. To see more of his work, visit youngalby.com, or email youngalby@yahoo.com.

Tea Benduhn is formerly an associate editor at *Bead&Button* magazine. Contact her in care of Kalmbach Books.

Kimberly Berlin is a full-time jewelry artist, teaches wireworking classes in San Antonio, Texas, and is the author of *Build Your Own Wire Pendants*. Contact Kimberly at berlik@flash.net.

Jimmie Boatright is a retired school teacher and lifelong crafter who teaches jewelry making at the Atlanta Bead Market in Buford, Ga. Contact her by phone at (678) 714-8293 or via email at atlantabeadmarket@hotmail.com, or see a list of her classes at atlantabeadmarket.com.

April Bradley lives in Valley Forge, Pa., with her husband and children. Contact April at april_bradley@comcast.net, or view her website, aprilbradley.com.

Angela Casaccio has been designing jewelry for about 10 years. She loves to make pieces with wire, chain, gemstones, and crystals. See more of her work at celacreations.com, or read her blog at celacreations.blogspot.com.

Lilian Chen's jewelry designs have been featured in several magazines, and her pieces have been recognized as finalists and semi-finalists in the Bead Dreams and Swarovski Create Your Style competitions. To see more of her designs, visit community.webshots.com/user/luckyperidot88, or email lilian888crystals@yahoo.com.

Anna Elizabeth Draeger is a former associate editor for *Bead&Button* magazine, and the author of *Crystal Brilliance, Great Designs for Shaped Beads*, and *Crystal Play*. Since 2009, she has been an ambassador for Create Your Style with Swarovski Elements. Her website is originaldesignsbyanna.squarespace.com.

Stephanie Eddy is a jewelry designer and teacher with more than 40 years of experience. Stephanie sells kits on her website, stephanieeddy.com. Contact Stephanie via e-mail at kitsforsale@stephanieeddy.com.

Jessica Fehrmann lives in West Bend, Wis. Contact her via e-mail at jessyemt@yahoo.com.

Leah Hanoud has been beading for 15 years and has a B.F.A. with a concentration in jewelry and metalsmithing from the University of Massachusetts. Contact Leah at (508) 677-1877 or turq2000@turquoise-stringbeads.com, or visit turquoise-stringbeads.com.

Jonna Ellis Holston is a full-time beader and teacher of beaded arts both privately and as a faculty member at the Sawtooth School of Visual Arts in Winston-Salem, N.C. You can contact her at gianabijou@yahoo.com.

Maria Kirk of Nottingham, England, designs, teaches, and creates kits. In 1999, one of her pieces was selected to adorn the Royal Christmas Tree at Buckingham Palace, and in 2009 she designed a crystal poppy to raise funds for the Royal British Legion Poppy Appeal. Contact her at maria@nostalgiaribbon.com or visit nostalgiabeads.com.

Kara Jacob uses beads to find the beauty in everyday life. Email Kara at harvest918@aol.com.

Jeka Lambert enjoys the challenge of solving design and structure problems. Every year, she designs and teaches 12–15 new projects near her home in Albany, Calif. Contact Jeka in care of Kalmbach Books.

Cathy Lampole of Newmarket, in Ontario, Canada, enjoys the fine detail that can be achieved with beadweaving, especially with crystals. Besides designing jewelry, Cathy owns a bead shop, That Bead Lady. Visit thatbeadlady.com, or e-mail her at cathy@thatbeadlady.com.

Shirley Lim resides in Singapore and has been beading since 2000. Contact Shirley at info@beading-fantasy.com, view beading-fantasy.com, or read beading-fantasy.blogspot.com.

Sharilyn Miller is a jewelry instructor and author of 11 books on jewelry making, including the Arty Jewelry ebook series. Visit her blog at sharilynmiller.blogspot.com or her website, sharilynmiller.com.

Cindy Pankopf teaches nationally at various venues including the Bead&Button Show and at her shop, Creative Place, in Fullerton, Cal. She is also a Master Instructor with Art Clay World USA. Cindy is the author of *BeadMaille* and *The Absolute Beginners Guide: Making Metal Clay Jewelry*. Visit her website, cpcreativeplace.com, or email her at info@cindypankopf.com.

Ludmila Raitzin is a renowned fashion designer featured in Saks Fifth Avenue, Neiman Marcus, and Bloomingdales. Her work has been exhibited in the Museum of Art and Design and has been published in several books and magazines. Contact her at raitzinl@yahoo.com.

Jean Ann Reeves has been beading most of her life, beginning with stringing buttons from her mother's button box. Contact her via email at buyalot6@aol.com, or visit etsy.com/shop/jewelrygeniebyjean.

Maggie Roschyk is a contributor to *Bead&Button* magazine and the author of *Artistic Seed Bead Jewelry*, published by Kalmbach Books. You can contact Maggie through her blog at BeadAndButton.com/MaggiesMusings.

Lynne Soto teaches her original designs and beading techniques in the Milwaukee area. Contact her at mscalto2@att.net.

Helene Tsigistras lives in Brookfield, Wis. She has been designing bead jewelry for years and is a regular contributor to *Bead&Button* magazine. Helene expresses her creative side by designing simple and elegant jewelry. Contact her in care of Kalmbach Books.

Jenny Van is a frequent contributor of popular *Bead&Button* crystal designs. Contact her at (714) 848-5626, email jenny@beadsj.com, or view her website, jjbead.com.

Lesley Weiss is the author of *The Absolute Beginners Guide: Stitching Beaded Jewelry* and is a former associate editor for *Bead&Button* magazine. Visit her website, homemade-handmade.net.

Stacy Werkheiser is an associate editor for *Bead&Button* magazine and the current editor of *Wirework* magazine. Contact her at swerkheiser@beadandbutton.com.

Kat West lives in Bremerton, Wash. She enjoys the meditative aspect of beading and believes creativity is essential to one's mental health. Visit Kat's website, kwbeads.com, or contact her at katwestbeads@gmail.com.

Wendy Witchner is a wire and metal jewelry artist who travels the United States in her motor home to sell her creations at art shows. Her work is also available at select galleries. Visit her website, wendywitchner-jewelrycom.

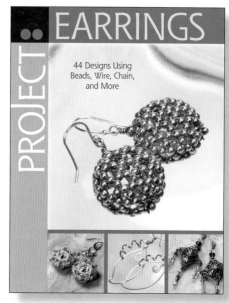